'What people are saying ab

"If you are a woman, who longs to lead a truly fulfilling life, I strongly encourage you to read Warrior Women - it will be as empowering as having a life-changing conversation with an exceptionally wise, warm and loving friend. The courage and compassion of its author shines through every page. Reading this empowering treasure trove of transformative wisdom will truly assist women to reclaim their spiritual courage and allow them to step into their true magnificence."

Jason Chan, Author 'Radiant Warrior' (Hay House 2009)
www.lightfoundation.co.uk

"This book - will change your life. It offers both practical help and advice and spiritual guidance to find your own energy source. It will help you design the life you really want and then show you how to live it. It will open your eyes to the endless possibilities that life has for you and empower you with the confidence to go and be the person you are meant to be. The stories of the Warrior Women are truly inspirational and will give hope to those who are struggling to find their way."

Edwina Silver, Founder of The Connexion – Networking for Women in Business.

"WOW! A truly brilliant book that gently encourages women to really look at their lives from a new perspective – that of being kind to yourself in everything you do. It teaches you to find your authentic self; the true power you have in your core.

This is a book about self- awareness; being able to see when enough is enough, and when stress is pushing you to breaking point. It shows you when you are rooted in negative fears and helps you move on from that destructive place. It explains the connection between self-worth and money – a feeling that you thoroughly deserve it.

Warrior Women is a lovely mix of the author's personal experiences and the courage of real life women who have overcome personal adversities. Every woman has come to a place of peace through clearing away non-serving beliefs, being kinder to themselves and being able to shine their own personal light out into the world.

From a place of love and kindness, Liz draws out the natural brilliance of women so they may easily and gracefully become true Warrior Women."

Amanda Goldston, Author of forthcoming book *'How to Manifest a Million – Cash'*

"I believe that a real understanding of human nature is often born out of adversity - through the challenges that she has faced and overcome Liz delivers her message with great compassion. As the reader, I immediately knew I could trust her guidance. The principles found within Warrior Women bring ancient wisdom to the modern age."

Ian Tucker, Author and Speaker *'Your Simple Path'*
www.iantucker.co.uk

"This book, written from the heart, shares extremely moving life stories that will resonate with women who would not normally consider 'self-help books'. The author encourages a change to thought processes that can help women feel better and more able to make significant improvements to their lives. It will especially benefit women that hold remnants of guilt and shame from relationship break- ups, problems with addiction or abuse and serves to remind all women they are never alone."

Lindsey Knott

"I instantly identified with this book and know many people who will benefit from Warrior Women. Liz revealed aspects of her life I never knew and feel amazed by her power to turn life around to the Joy and Abundance she now lives in. Using my network, I hope to share this magnificence and see the KindnessCODE develop into the recognised brand it truly deserves to be. My dream is to be part of the journey and help people realise theirs..."

Nikki Howard

"This book brings hope and the possibility for women, from all walks of life, to take control of their lives by changing their perspective and taking positive steps to treat themselves with kindness and respect.

Although some of the topics in Warrior Women may have been covered in some way by other writers, Liz brings a new depth to the way she talks about our level of consciousness and the interconnectedness that is humanity. I believe any woman reading this book will definitely find something that resonates with them.

The mixture of humour, theoretical and scientific concepts, gently yet probing questions and opportunities to stop and reflect, makes Warrior Women not only a useful resource for women, but an enjoyable and engaging read too!"

Oenca Fontaine, Author *'My God in a Time Like Now'*

"Every woman needs to read 'Warrior Women'. I feel inspired and empowered and already I want to read it again. Packed with energy, love and such powerful words this book has become my new 'bible'. Something I can live by and refer to. If I keep this in my heart and head, life will be truly rich."

Suz Jarman

WARRIOR WOMEN

HOW TO BE **MAGNIFICENT** THROUGH THE **COURAGE** OF **SELF KINDNESS**

LIZ KEANEY

WARRIOR WOMEN

www.lizkeaney.com

ISBN 978-1-907308-11-6

First published in Great Britain by Compass Publishing 2015.

A catalogue record of this book is available from the British Library.

Set and designed by The Book Refinery Ltd.

Dedicated with love

To the Warrior Women featured in this book for their trust and friendship. Thank you Alison, Sue, Jules, Kaitlyn, Vicky, Nikki and Hayley – you are amazing.

To the women, past and ongoing, that have participated in the 'Why and Worth' workshops –with special thanks to Sue, Jacky, Hang, Gill and Dina for being there from the start; your feedback, enthusiasm and vision got me here.
You are a special group of Warriors.

To my husband John, for your unconditional love, support and belief.

To my Mom and Dad, Margaret and John, for everything you have shown me.

To my sister and best friend, Jane you always make me smile

And thank you to everyone that has touched my life to date. We are all connected.

Contents

Contents

PART FOUR ~ Energy

PART FIVE ~ True Stories

Foreword

Please do not underestimate the value of the message in this book, because Liz had to nearly die in order to gain the understanding that she will be sharing here with you...

A quote I often use with my clients is, *"do you learn from others mistakes or do you insist on making your own."* ~ Richard Wilkins.

Please 'choose' to learn all you can from Liz's mistakes (lessons), as these can offer you a priceless short cut to what's truly important, which is the relationship with yourself.

This must be the foundation for everything else that exists in your life and when you *'dare to put your own oxygen mask on first'* you will become fully energised to be the best you that you can possibly be, in turn you will be an example of this to others which will help everyone around you...your family, your friends and all of the people you want to help the most.

You see, *"nothing can, nothing ever will exceed the relationship you have with yourself."*

Why?

Because you won't allow it to.

So many of us don't believe that we truly deserve what we actually want and if you don't believe you deserve it, then you won't allow it to manifest in your life

This book will change your life!!!

... but only if you allow it to...

The only thing that can prevent this from happening is if you continue to listen to and believe that negative voice in your head. This voice is a liar, and the way to prove this to yourself is to do the things that Liz recommends in the book - even when the voice in your head tells you that you can't.

Hear that voice and do it anyway.

The consequences of this will change your entire life from the inside out...

I salute you in advance Warrior Woman for your courage to *'be'* and *'to love'* who you truly are.

This is not only a wonderful gift to yourself but also a much needed gift to our world

The Dalai Lama said, *"That the western woman will change the world."*

And we will do this, firstly by honouring and valuing ourselves, secondly by extending this same kindness to others, then through collaboration we will share this love and kindness from our hearts which will create an external world that we can all feel extremely proud of...what an incredible legacy.

As Liz so rightly explains throughout the book, this journey all begins and ends with *you being kinder* and more loving *to yourself.*

Sent with love from my heart ♥ to yours ♥.

Elizabeth Ivory

The Ministry Of Inspiration and Author of *'It's Not Your Fault!: Because You're Not Choosing'.*

Introduction

Modern day women set high expectations. They feel they need to be the best partner, mother, daughter, domestic goddess, career woman, and a bedroom siren to boot. But with these expectations, many women are finding it more and more difficult to raise their hands and say, *"help, I can't do all this".*

Why?

Because for many women, this means admitting to being vulnerable, which is linked with feelings of weakness, guilt and shame. For some, not asking for help may result in breakdown, depression, exhaustion, abuse, low self-esteem, addiction and relationships issues.

This book is about regular women who have had courage: courage to be kind to themselves by acknowledging their vulnerability, making it public and connecting with their authentic self.

These are women you will easily relate to, women whose challenges have opened a new door in their life. These are women who are living life on purpose with purpose. They are living in their truth, even if this has not always presented the quickest or the most lucrative answers. These are women who have searched for meaning in their life, and along the way have become more in tune with their body, mind and soul.

My reason for writing this book is to inspire women like you to be kinder to yourself. I want to stop you beating yourself up with self-sabotaging behaviour and self-judgment. I also want to encourage you to view your life with kind sight and have the courage to reveal your vulnerabilities. If you connect to the truth of who you really are, you will step into the unique magnificence of you already are.

Who Is The Warrior?

If you had been with me five years ago, on December 15, you would have witnessed me open my front door and welcome my visitor inside.

He turned up at 7pm as arranged, and as he hobbled over my doorstep, clearly in great discomfort, he randomly asked: *"Who is the warrior?"*

I didn't realise the significance of his question at the time, and didn't know that the word warrior was about to change lives forever.

I laughed off my visitor's question and led him through the hallway to my extension, a peaceful room that backs on to the garden. He had come to me to see if I could help alleviate some discomfort in his leg, an irritating pain he'd had for several weeks. Although senior in years, he was very young at heart and this pain was preventing him from getting out and about and enjoying the freedom and pastimes of his retirement. Forty-five minutes later, the pain had gone and he was walking down my drive, somewhat incredulous over this new freedom of movement.

What happened the next day was kind of spooky. My neighbours had just had a new kitchen installed and were proudly showing me their new cupboards and appliances. As I walked around admiring the newness and shininess of it all, they drew my attention to their replaced slate flooring. It was greyish black with flecks of silver and white.

My neighbour pulled me towards a specific tile and asked: *"Can you see what we can see?"*

As a child, did you do that thing where you stared at trees, clouds, or perhaps the moon, to see if you could see the images of faces, animals and things? It wasn't cold in my neighbours' kitchen, but as I stared at this specific tile, I shivered. Immediately, I saw what they could see. Through the flecks of silver and white there was an image similar to the profile of a warrior – like a Red Indian with a feathered headdress. As I nodded in agreement, my neighbour fetched a book from his lounge and explained that he'd been reading all about the history of our area. This book described a meeting place - *the Red Warrior Club* - that had once existed on the road we live in. We all laughed at the coincidence.

Have you ever heard or seen a word or an object, and then kept hearing and seeing other things that reconnect you with it? For example, it is a bit like ordering a new car and then seeing exactly the same make, model and colour everywhere you go. It leads you to wonder why everyone just went out and bought the same car as you. Bizarrely, the words warriors, tribes and feathers kept coming to my attention. I wondered if it was a coincidence, or was there a subtle message for me?

I thought for a long time about the word *Warrior*. It's an English word with a masculine, fighting charge to it, but the more I delved into its true definition, the more I learned that the ancient interpretation was less about violence, power and strength and more about kindness, courage and connection. I knew nothing about Red Indians, but I discovered that the Native Americans tenets were about representing honour, integrity and truth.

> *"The Warrior is not someone who fights.*
> *The true warrior has engaged in struggle;*
> *the battle is not fighting but rather a personal battle*
> *to perfect character, to become the best in every area*
> *of life with honour and character in peace*
> *and benevolence."*
> *Chief Sitting Bull of the Sioux Tribe*

Perhaps my mind did go into overdrive, but I decided to look a bit more deeply into Native American culture. I discovered that women, like their men, wore feathers as a symbolic representation of their courage. Note that I said *courage*, not strength - I'll come back to that. They respected each tribe's autonomy, and their values were collaboration, reciprocity and balance.

Women wore red face paint to demonstrate beauty and happiness. Red was considered a sacred colour, a colour of warmth that illuminated protection, creation and ritualistic traditions. It was also a colour of the emotions of the heart: love, passion and fire. Fires were lit to connect them to a spiritual power, an intention that sent healing prayers to the Great Spirit. Fires were also symbolic of the cleansing and renewal of life. Out of ashes came new growth, thoughts and ideas. They communicated their thoughts through painted symbols and signs, which depicted their purpose, vision and faith – their beliefs.

It made me think.

Modern day life seldom encourages us to open our minds and align ourselves with the energies of the Great Spirit, God, or the Universe in the same way that other ancient cultures did. I don't necessarily mean we should follow a religion, but it's good for us to consciously be in harmony with the elements and the source of creation, such as Mother Earth and the beauty of light and colour. I will refer to this generally as the Universe. You can find your own word.

Perhaps this may be a new concept to you, but I remember hearing the phrase:

> *Your mind is like a parachute – it works best when it is open.*

So what happened after the kitchen tile incident? Well, there were lots of synchronicities. I found feathers lodged by my front door and on my car, and other events occurred that made me wonder if these were signs telling me that I needed to understand more about Warriors.

The penny dropped some weeks after the visit from the gentleman with the leg pain. I realised the answer to his question. Maybe I was the Warrior by living my life on purpose, with purpose, sharing my vision and empowering others to find their own magnificence through a CODE of self-kindness. Maybe it was no coincidence then that I started meeting many wonderful women. Not extraordinary women, just regular women like you who had experienced life.

Through the ups and downs of life, these women had all gained an appreciation of the importance of self-nurture, self-worth and self-connection. They shared values of honour and integrity and were empowered by an inner trust and confidence. This was their perfection of character. Not a vain or arrogant perfection, but a simple harmony - an alignment with a more defined purpose, vision and belief.

But more significantly, these women had revealed an emotional vulnerability that required courage, and an openness to remove the modern mask of strength that we often hide behind: a mask that can keep feelings and emotions hidden.

By revealing their real feelings, confronting their inner beliefs and facing their fears, they found their true self. This gave them freedom from self-limitation and they discovered a depth and knowledge that might be considered *'out there'.* This concerned non-material worlds, the metaphysical (abstract concepts such as time and space), energy vibration, the law of attraction and states of mind. Their truth gave them a path of reason or understanding (you might call it spirituality), and through this they began to have an understanding of *'why'* they were here and what their purpose and *'worth'* - self-worth - was. Through understanding their why and worth they had stepped into their magnificence.

I call them Warrior Women.

> *"A master warrior has character, wisdom and insight."*
> Forrest E. Morgan ~ Author of 'Living the Martial Way:
> A manual for the way a modern warrior should think'

I believe that the values revealed by the Warrior Women in this book have not changed from those displayed by the Native Americans. Each woman is on a journey to be a leader, a luminary and a change maker. They may not fit the typical image of a suited and booted leader, but these are women who embrace their feminine energy (without necessarily being feminists). They see the value in collaborating (not competing) with others. They recognise that life is a balance of giving and receiving. *Warrior Women* have a connection with the earth and its elements, and with an unseen energy. Above all, they have a connection with who they really are. Through changing their belief patterns, they have taken responsibility for their lives and have allowed themselves to recognise their own significance and magnificence. This isn't a vain or arrogant magnificence, it's simply that they understand their greatness and potential.

My intention is that this book will encourage you to remove your mask of strength, which will give you the courage to confront your non-serving inner beliefs and feel inspired to see your life with a new perspective. It will give you an awareness of how much you value yourself, your self-nurture, your self-worth and your self-connection. This is an awareness that I refer to as consciousness. Through this you will see that you can be the healer of your own life. With this consciousness may you live an inspired life of health, joy and abundance, and in doing so start a healing ripple, creating a legacy of magnificence for all those you touch.

"Our deepest fear is not that we are inadequate. Our deepest fear is that we are powerful beyond measure. It is our light, not our darkness that most frightens us. We ask ourselves, who am I to be brilliant, gorgeous, talented, fabulous? Actually, who are you not to be? You are a child of God. Your playing small does not serve the world. There is nothing enlightened about shrinking so that other people won't feel insecure around you. We are all meant to shine, as children do. We were born to make the glory of God that is within us. It's not just in some of us; it's in everyone. And as we let our own light shine, we unconsciously give other people permission to do the same. As we are liberated from our own fear, our presence automatically liberates others."
From 'A Return to Love' by Marianne Williamson ~ Spiritual Teacher, Author and Lecturer

Finding the Warrior Within

Perhaps the day I first (unknowingly) stepped into becoming a Warrior was the day I decided to seek some answers. It was the fateful or blessed day (depending on your perspective) that my second cancer diagnosis was confirmed. I couldn't believe that this was happening to me again. It was only six months since I'd recovered from a major operation and endured some particularly unpleasant and invasive treatment.

Now this.

The nurse, in her starched blue uniform, described the protocol to me. Handing me a leaflet she explained, as kindly as she could, that I would need another operation as well as more radiotherapy and chemotherapy. And yes, there would be sickness, and - oh joy - my hair would fall out...blah, blah, blah.

If you had been with me that day, you'd have known I wasn't really hearing her words. I felt extremely nauseous and faint and the room was spinning into a whirl of blue, yellow and green. If it wasn't for the chair I was sat on, I surely would have been flat on the floor. I heard the quiver in my own voice as I asked the nurse a question.
 "Why me? What have I done to deserve this again?"
 She placed her hand on my shoulder and in a reassuring voice replied: *"My dear, don't blame yourself. You have done nothing to deserve this."*
 At that very moment, the room suddenly stopped spinning and everything became still. Then I heard a reply to my question. The reply didn't come from the nurse, but I was acutely aware that there was no one else in the room. I recognised the voice. I knew it really well. It was my own voice and it spoke silently in my head.

I'll tell you what my voice said...later.

Fifteen minutes on, still feeling shaky on my feet, I walked with jelly legs out of the hospital. Despite the August sunshine, I was shivering inside and out, still numb with shock. As I made my way down the pedestrian exit back to my car something weird happened.

First, it was the flowers.

The petals in the large ceramic pots in the car park entrance suddenly jumped right out at me. Their colour danced right in front of my eyes, their magenta velvety softness coming alive in a vibrant blast like a magnificent 3D picture. Except it wasn't a picture. This was real life.

Then it was the trees. Of course, the trees had always been there, but today was different. How was it that I'd never noticed before that there were 101 different shades of green? Just for a moment I stopped and focused on a leaf. I was sure that I could see it breathing.

Quiet, be still. I listened...

Unusually, there was no traffic on the road in front of the car park exit, and rising above the silence I could hear the birds singing. God, what was happening? *"Get a grip, Liz!"* I thought. You've seen flowers, trees and heard birds singing before - after all, you've been around for quite a few decades now. But I knew this day was unique. It was unique because I wanted everything to be in slow motion. I wanted to savour every moment, to be really aware and conscious of my surroundings. I needed to make doubly sure that I was still here, and I needed to really feel and value this moment in my life. I wanted to listen, not simply hear. I wanted to see, not simply look. In that moment, I was aware that the double blow, two cancer diagnoses in 12 months, was now a wake-up call. It was the opportunity for me to wake up and see the beauty in my life: not just the beauty of the flowers and the trees, but the complete beauty and perspective of everything. I didn't realise it then, but this would also mean seeing the beauty of being kind to myself.

The house I lived in was lovely and the locality was affluent and polite, but right then that mattered less. My company car with the convertible roof was a bonus, but it didn't matter. The job and salary was very nice, but what price do you put on health? What mattered was that I was here. I was alive and I wanted to carry on being alive. No, I didn't want to just be alive, I wanted to start feeling alive; living and breathing every moment with energy, zest and vitality. I was overwhelmed with a deep gratitude that I was here and could see the flowers and trees and hear the birds. Suddenly, I was acutely aware that my typical corporate everyday busy life, which involved rushing here and there, had robbed me of my awareness of the things that have always been there: those little things that make us smile...if we only take time to notice. Take for instance the toddler in his buggy being wheeled by his mother in my direction. As they passed me by, the little boy grinned widely. I didn't just see his smile, I really felt it, too. In that brief moment, I allowed myself the time to connect with the little boy's beaming grin. Then I felt my own inner smile - it was in my heart.

> *"Slow down and enjoy life. It's not just the scenery*
> *you miss by going too fast – you also miss the sense*
> *of where you are going and why."*
> Eddie Cantor ~ US Entertainer and Author

I couldn't help but think that there he was with the rest of his life in front of him. He was too young to have developed any concerns for the next minute, day or year of his life. As I got closer to my car, I wondered - what is this thing called life? What is this thing called life but a series of seconds, minutes, hours, days, weeks, months and years that equal time? Life was simply an interpretation of time.

Despite feeling a bit wobbly, I couldn't help but smile at the paradox. Only the day before, in my corporate job, I'd sat through a long training presentation on time management. I'd been restless and fidgety, willing for the trainer to get on with it. After all, I had urgent things to sort out, phone calls to return and emails to answer. I'd returned to work six months earlier (following my cancer treatment) and was back in the groove of corporate responsibility, competition, targets, expectations and hiding behind the title on my business card. Back on automatic pilot, I was wearing the mask of coping, and kept my upper lip stiff. The mask meant I could seldom cry, admit discord or reveal vulnerability.

Although I had little interest in the time management presentation, I suddenly remembered something that the trainer had said: *"There is no such thing as time management, only SELF management"*.

Managing Myself

As I opened my car door, I pondered on the significance of those words. What if the interpretation of my life - very significantly my health - was all about managing my SELF?

In that moment, I made a decision. Just for today, I was going to manage myself. I was going to please myself and make 'me' my priority. I was going to be kinder to myself, too. I didn't know how specifically, but I knew I had to find some answers.

People said: *"That's weird, you did what?"*

I drove to the library as it seemed a good place to start. It was easy to locate books on health and wellness and I had a hunch that I could start being kinder with what I put in my body. I scoured the shelves for books on food and nutrition and was amazed at the vast choice. Thrilled I could borrow 12 books at a time, I amused myself trying to carry all of them without dropping one. (Note to self: next time, take a carrier bag.)

Once home, my brain couldn't devour the science within these books fast enough. Within hours, my living room floor was covered with copious notes I'd made about which foods help promote health and which hinder it. Pretty soon, I was in a groove of learning. Most days I could be found in the library or bookshop trying to fulfil my newfound hunger for knowledge. Reading became hugely empowering. This is because the more I learned about how I could help myself, the less I felt like a passive participant of my diagnosis, a victim if you will. I realised that I could still go ahead and have the conventional treatment on offer, but I could involve myself and take part in my own wellness at the same time. This new approach would allow me to make adjustments to my life that would help me deal with my cancer positively.

The scientific jigsaw of how an inappropriate diet can exacerbate stress and increase vulnerability to illness started to make sense to me. Alarmingly, it became very evident that with my demanding corporate job, I was perpetuating my own stress with my diet. I'd got into the habit of eating on the go, skipping meals, relying on convenience foods and having no regard for nutritional value. I was eating simply to fill a gap, and realised that I could be a whole lot kinder to myself with what I ate. It was time to embark on some serious self-nurture.

Fast-forward a few weeks. Once again, I was browsing for more books on nutritional health - only something was different. To this day, I don't know what made me turn around and look at the shelf to the side of me. A book, with its blue and white spine, was leaning out. Someone hadn't put it back on the shelf properly. Impulsively, I lifted it from its place. As I did so, I looked up and noticed with horror that the sign above this shelf was labelled SELF-HELP in big, bold letters.

Self-help

OMG, this was embarrassing, almost shameful. Here I was, suited and booted, en route to an appointment for my corporate job. I didn't fit the profile of flaky or helpless, or, for that matter, a hippy or simply a bit 'woo woo'. I was most definitely not the sort of person that would have publicly acknowledged that I needed help.

Did I really need help?

I checked that no one was looking before guardedly reading the back cover of the book. The words described one man's amazing journey back to complete wellness after being diagnosed with an incurable degenerative disease. His diagnosis was not mine, but I was intrigued nevertheless. However, my rational mind stepped in, trying to get the better of me. I thought surely that's not possible - people don't heal from something that serious, do they? Curiosity got the better of me. I hid the book in my black and very important looking faux leather corporate folder while I walked to the till to pay. After all, it was a self-help book!

I'm sure you've heard people say that a random quote, poem or song changed their life. Well, I'd like to tell you that this book changed my life, but that wouldn't be the complete truth. However, I will give it huge credit for being the catalyst that set me on the path to changing my life. Why? Because this book gave me a new awareness. I will refer to this as a consciousness. This encouraged me to focus on what health I did have, not the other way round. It invited me to have gratitude for my physical body and all the things I could do. After all, I could still breathe, walk, talk, see, hear, smell and touch. I could still read, write, drive, iron, vacuum and use a keyboard. I started noticing the people in my everyday life who weren't as lucky as me and, funnily enough, once I took my consciousness to it, I started noticing them everywhere. People who were using wheelchairs or were blind or missing arms and legs. Or people who couldn't walk a flight of stairs without being really breathless. Every time I took my awareness to someone like that, it took me out of a place of feeling sorry for myself and into a place of feeling blessed. I was grateful for the health I did have.

The book helped me to see my body as a place of nurture that I could feed kindly, not only with food, but also with kind thoughts. It also introduced a new reality, one where I saw my body as more than a collection of its parts and anatomy systems. I saw it as an energetic field that was within me and radiated from me. The book also opened my eyes to the possibility that there could be a connection between my physical body and my emotions. It suggested my mind was in my heart, not in my head.

Are you joking?

> **"When the student is ready the teacher appears."**
> ~ *Old theosophical statement*

Now, if I'm truthful, the book didn't make much sense at first, but nevertheless I couldn't deny that it was very inspirational. So much so, that I started seeking similar books, ones that didn't just deal with the science of the body. These were books that explained mind, body and spirit connections as well as mind mastery and energy awareness. Gosh, I surprised myself. I loved this self-help stuff and whenever I got the opportunity, I'd be back in the bookshop or library searching for books that could inspire me even more, and perhaps even help me find some answers regarding my health diagnosis.

Something within me told me that I needed to take responsibility and be a player in my own wellness. The more I read, the more answers I found.

"To be teachable we need to know what it is we are seeking." ~ Old proverb

The little voice

Oh, I nearly forgot to tell you what happened that day in hospital...the day I heard the voice in my head. Remember, I'd asked the nurse the question, *"Why me, what have I done to deserve this?"* The voice I recognised as my own voice posed a question/statement. It was without blame or accusation, it simply said: *"Just suppose if you had played some part in this, then just suppose you could play a part in undoing it."*

That was eight years ago.

Today I enjoy a fabulous new perspective on life and possess health, happiness and wealth. I cannot NOT share everything I learned on this journey. I feel compelled to pass on everything I know about self-nurture, self-worth and self-connection, as well as what I've learned about the link between science, our senses and our soul. I also want to share everything I discovered along the way about nutrition and stress, cause and effect, mind mastery, emotional freedom, self-development, energy psychology, qigong and the mind-body connection. All of these are labels, labels for something I now refer to as the **KindnessCODE**.

I want to make it clear that I don't have all the answers – who does? I also know that there may be imperfections in this book and that's OK, because this isn't a book about being perfect. What is perfect anyway? It's a book about stepping into being magnificent without perfection. I got on and wrote the book from my heart because I want to share the message that YOU matter. The interpretation of your life has a direct correlation with the level of self-kindness you afford yourself.

The KindnessCODE is for you if you:

✓ Feel that the hamster wheel of life is getting faster and faster. You feel like you're swimming in treacle, spinning all the plates as you try to get it all done.

✓ Drive yourself crazy by comparing yourself to others. Set yourself exacting standards of perfection personally or professionally, or feel that you are constantly being judged.

✓ Feel resentful that others monopolise your time. You feel drained by the way other people burden you with their problems.

✓ Feel unappreciated or undervalued. Others treat you with disrespect and take you for granted. Perhaps you find yourself saying yes when you mean no.

✓ Feel low in energy and shattered at the end of every week. You have the feeling that the proverbial straw might break the camel's back any day soon.

✓ Are trying to conform to someone else's expectations of you. You feel judged, inadequate and not good enough. You find yourself saying, *"I should"* or, *"I ought"* a bit too often.

✓ Feel trapped in a life that is no longer your own. Perhaps your relationship or job is past its sell-by date? You are stuck, but the thought of moving on is just too scary.

✓ Want to hide from the world. Life seems to have lost its joy and there are more low days than highs.

✓ Are newly single (maybe divorced, separated or widowed), or your kids have now flown the nest. You have lost sight of who you really are and where you are going in life. You'd like a greater sense of purpose and identity.

✓ Feel that you are wearing a mask most of the time, which is hiding the real you. This mask outwardly says *"I'm OK"* but deep down you're lacking in confidence, have low self-esteem and are plagued by anxiety and *'what if'* questions.

✓ You face a health challenge.

The **KindnessCODE** is a four-part process to help you incorporate more self-compassion into your life without guilt. Through understanding the CODE you will unravel your why and worth. Your *'why'* will tell you the reason stuff happens to you. When you understand the profound truth of this you can change the blueprint of your life. In doing so, you will have a clearer vision of your purpose and can raise your expectations. Life's riches will be for the taking because you'll discover that you are *'worth it'*.

Imagine how good it would feel to be able to:

★ Loosen your grip on life, slow down and have time for yourself.

★ Really like and love yourself (without arrogance or vanity) and be respected, loved and adored.

★ Have freedom from self-limitation.

★ Be calm and confident in any situation.

★ Have a clear vision for what you want in life and believe you deserve it.

★ Step into the unique magnificence of who you really are.

It is my privilege to share the **KindnessCODE** with you. This code has unleashed the richness of my life, my health, my joy and my abundance. My wish is that it does the same for you.

Follow the **KindnessCODE** and become a *Warrior Woman.*

 PART ONE

Consciousness

When you understand Part One, you'll wonder how you have managed to live your life with your eyes open yet have seen so little. It is absolutely pivotal to understanding the relevance of the rest of the CODE.

*Part one is the **C** in the **CODE**, which stands for **Consciousness.** This involves being mindful and aware of the limitations that you may have imposed on your own self-compassion.*

Living Life Consciously

Until you embrace Part One, you will never be the captain of your ship and will unwittingly impede your magnificence

Unless you live on planet Zog, you already understand the meaning of the word kindness. I believe that most people in the world have the capacity to be kind. But my question is: how easy do you find it to be kind to yourself?

I bet if I were to step into your life for a day I'd see that your life is busy. I'm sure I'd see you trying to keep all the plates spinning as well as juggling all the balls in the air. It no longer matters whether you live in a tranquil village or a noisy city - life is full on. I expect you see your mobile phone or tablet as an invaluable accessory that instantly connects you with what is going on in the world, be that 10 yards or 10,000 miles away, and you would feel lost without it. As great as technology is, it's possible that you feel you are on an information overload: news, TV, radio, adverts, marketing, emails and social media pervade your day. I'm sure you can't have helped but notice that everyone, including you, is in a rush. I call this Hurry Syndrome. Everyone is rushing to accomplish everything in double quick time. Fast-track at the supermarket, fast-track at the airport. Many of the emails in your inbox have an air of urgency about them, or a subliminal message of lack if you don't act by a certain date. I guess there will be days when you feel overwhelmed by the demands of life. There is so much to do and seldom enough time to do it in. So many people or situations require your attention, and there are so many individuals to please. I expect you know someone who has such a frantic life that she rarely has time to think about what to prepare for dinner. Does she find it easier to rely on convenience foods or send out for fast-food delivery? You might be the woman who seldom takes a break for lunch or eats on the go, and if you do it's to satiate hunger pangs rather than nurture yourself. Perhaps your life is like a hamster wheel running at a zillion miles an hour. But does the breakneck speed of life mean that self-kindness often eludes you?

It's possible that you fall prey to coughs, colds or flare-ups a bit too often. Maybe you cannot shift those unwanted pounds or often feel totally knackered.

Ask yourself this: *in your busy-ness, how often do you take time out to be kind to you?* I don't mean buying a new pair of shoes, handbag or having your nails done (not that there's anything wrong with that), I mean a real internal kindness that requires putting yourself first.

Are you always saying, *"I haven't got time?"*

Q. *How guilty do you feel about making time for you?*

Put Your Oxygen Mask On First

Admittedly, it was many years ago now, but I still remember the first time I travelled on an aeroplane. The cabin crew delivered the safety drill and I can vividly recall feeling quite aghast when they said, *"In case of an emergency, fit your own oxygen mask before fitting your child's."* It seemed wrong to me. Why wouldn't you put your child first? These days, it makes perfect sense to me. If you stop breathing, you're brown bread. You're no help to anyone if you're dead, which is why you have to put yourself first and put that oxygen mask on.

Your life from now on starts with YOU. See if you can suspend the belief that the remainder of your life has anything to do with your partner, family, friends, neighbours, community, town or government. It's YOU that matters, regardless of your age, size, colour, culture, education or upbringing. From this moment on, how about giving yourself permission to be kinder to yourself? Be kinder with how you nurture your body, feed your mind and understand the truth of who you really are.

Just for now, for this minute, I'd like you to know that it's perfectly OK to put yourself first.

"Oh no," can I hear you say? *"I can't do that. It's selfish."* You may be shaking your head because other people need you to be there for them. It may be your children, the elderly, colleagues, clients or customers. So let me be clear – this is not about neglecting those people who really depend on you. This isn't about being less kind to others. This is about understanding that your life needs to have balance, and it's absolutely right for you to have some respect for yourself, and for your time.

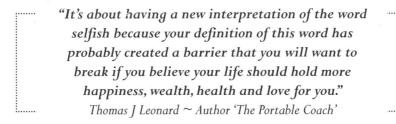

> *"It's about having a new interpretation of the word selfish because your definition of this word has probably created a barrier that you will want to break if you believe your life should hold more happiness, wealth, health and love for you."*
> Thomas J Leonard ~ Author 'The Portable Coach'

But before we move on, consider this:

Wearing the other mask

Are you open to the possibility that you or someone you know has a problem with an addiction?

The word may conjure up a relationship with drugs, alcohol, tobacco, sugar, chocolate, or even sex.

Let me keep the word '*addiction*', but when you read it mentally swap it for one of these words - habit, compulsion, enslavement.

Maybe that addiction (not yours, of course) could be to the TV, social media, surfing the net, overeating, overspending or keeping fit. Maybe someone you know is addicted to working long hours, perhaps through the urge to succeed or because of a fear of failure. Maybe they are addicted to people pleasing and are always complying with other people's wishes by saying, *"yes"* when they really mean *"no"*. Or maybe fear is causing them to say *"no"* when they really mean *"yes"*. Do you know someone who has an addiction to putting themselves down? Who is unable to accept compliments or praise? Or maybe you know someone who feels worthless and is self-harming, or is trying too hard to fit in. How about an addiction to blaming others or procrastinating over decisions? I expect you also know someone who lives their life on automatic pilot. They cope by distracting themselves from whatever emotion it is that they don't want to face.

What if they (or you) have become so used to living their life in any of the ways outlined above, that they constantly live with this compulsion, habit or enslavement? What if it's so below their radar that they don't even recognise it? But what if permanently wearing a mask and hiding their true self could potentially affect their wellness, happiness and wealth?

There is no judgment here: we all do it sometimes. But now might be a good time for me to share my lightbulb moment with you. The real meaning of disease:

> **Dis – ease**; *living your life out of ease/harmony with* **yourSELF**.

If you are most people, then you were fortunate enough to be born with two hands: left and right. These hands symbolise giving and receiving. So here is my question: *how much of your life to date has been spent giving time and energy to things or people that distract you from your SELF-management? How much of your life has been spent trying to please others? How hard do you find it to give yourself permission to receive some kindness for yourself?*

How many minutes in the day have you mastered as your time? This is time to live life on YOUR terms with some self-compassion. Now, just in case you think I'm implying that you need to make massive changes and drop everything here and now, I'm not. I'm simply referring to having awareness, a consciousness of how you are living your life and how much self-management you've afforded yourself. How much you value yourself and the life you live. Can you really be of service to others if you are running on empty?

Let's just remind ourselves of the aeroplane emergency drill. *"Please ensure you fix your own mask before attending to anyone else's."* Sort yourself out FIRST. So, just for now, let's suspend all previous interpretations and give the word selfish a new interpretation. What if, by firstly being kind to yourself, you could be more generous and supportive to others than you have ever been in your life?

WOW – *what an awesome concept.*

Several years ago, before my health challenges, my mind wasn't open enough to the possibility that this phrase could have any foundation. But today I know different. I will share with you how being kinder to yourself (selfish if you want) will allow you to be more generous, supportive and collaborative than you could imagine possible. You will also live your dream life and help others to do the same.

You can only truly help others if you help yourself first. Your health, happiness and wealth quotient is entirely the by-product of your own relationship with yourself, and that starts with an awareness, a consciousness that YOU matter. It's about you developing the qualities of self-management, self-responsibility and self-respect. It's about gaining self-belief and self-love. By the way, I don't mean vain or arrogant love here. I call it the **S E L F** principle. We'll come back to this later.

Once you have this consciousness you can start to believe that you are a player in your life and the captain of your ship. Seriously, I don't underestimate how much of a challenging concept this may be, especially when faced with a life threatening disease, a financial challenge, a relationship breakdown or even a job that sucks the very life out of you. But everything started to change for me on the day I took responsibility for myself. For now, I will have to ask you to trust me on this. It will become clearer as you progress through the book and become familiar with the Warrior Women stories.

Begin your journey of consciousness with your physical body by developing a greater awareness of what you are putting into it. I'd like to help you understand that as well as playing a part in your body image, food also affects your stamina, strength, growth and cell renewal, as well as your mental capacity: memory, concentration and mood. Food can help or hinder you in times of stress.

Before I started seeking answers to my health diagnosis, I thought I had a good knowledge of what represented healthy eating, but what I discovered completely changed my mind. I found out that as well as a pleasure, food is also energy. Now, this might sound a bit simplified and I know you already know that food is a fuel. The whole purpose of eating is to keep the body going. But it should also nurture every cell of the body. Consider the meaning of the word nutrition:

The process of providing or obtaining food necessary for health and growth.

You need regular, good quality fuel to replenish the cells in your body. This will help you to keep healthy and go the distance without illness and malaise. Would you only half-fill your petrol tank and then expect your car to keep running non-stop for hundreds of miles?

All food has a nutritional value, but the foods that tend to dominate the western diet, such as refined carbohydrates and processed foods, are exceptionally low on the nutritional scale. No wonder so many people feel low in energy. When I began having a body and food consciousness, I recognised that I had been less than kind to myself – this was not self-nurture. It became glaringly evident that missing meals or eating erratically meant that my energy ran out and tiredness and lethargy stepped in.

I discovered that I'd been misguided concerning the truth about sugar and fats, and I'd allowed myself to be duped by a diet industry that was making millions by keeping people overweight. Yes, you did read that correctly. I also found out that the five-a-day fruit/vegetable guidelines were woefully inadequate, especially for anyone dealing with a serious health challenge, and I was astounded that labels like natural, healthy and organic were sometimes only half-truths. I learned that many foods are cleverly marketed to come across as *'healthy'* when in fact they are the exact opposite with the potential to promote obesity, heart disease, blood sugar imbalances and inflammatory problems. It became very evident to me that the perpetuators and beneficiaries of many modern-day health issues are the food and pharmaceutical companies, which then sell a 'magic pill' to make everything better. There is no judgment here – drugs can serve a purpose, but my point is that you can take some responsibility for how you fuel your body. Don't cross your fingers and hope that a chemical/synthetic drug (with its potential side effects) is going to be your magic pill. It will only address the symptom, not the cause.

Q. How many people do you know who rely on a pill for a stress or health related symptom?

How Full Is Your Bath?

Stress is a word we all understand in modern day life. Can you feel it when you take your consciousness to it? Where are your shoulders positioned as you read this book? Are they tense and hunched at around chin level, or are they relaxed? Take your awareness to your bum cheeks. Are they clenched? What about your legs? Are your thigh muscles tensed? Are your legs pinched and crossed? Are you frowning or chewing your nails? Next time you get into your car, notice how tightly you grip the steering wheel. How quickly does your heartbeat increase when you think you might miss the bus or be late for an appointment?

How much of a challenge is it for you to simply sit or stand still without moving for a couple of minutes? How much does it test your patience to simply be with the consciousness of your breath and your heart beat? How often do you stop to listen to the breeze, the birds singing or gaze at the clouds?

Sit with me on the 5.20pm train back from London, a journey that I took last week. Two young women in my carriage were talking so loudly that it was easy to earwig on their conversation. From their banter, it was evident that they'd been on a girly shopping day out. The older of the two was complaining over and over about how stressed she was. They'd spent all day flitting in and out of department stores in Oxford Street and Knightsbridge and she still hadn't found the ideal shoes to compliment her new aqua blue cocktail dress. How difficult could it be to find the right ones? The only shoes she'd liked hadn't been available in her size. *"Why does this have to happen to me?"* she moaned, before remarking how flipping unhelpful the shop assistant had been. Now her feet were aching and she felt as though her head was going to explode. As she became more and more animated, her stress became palpable. The party was only five days away. When was she ever going to find time to look elsewhere? She convinced herself, out loud, that everybody at the party would look better than her and, of course, those bitch sisters, Pippa and Sophie, would be the first to point out that she wasn't wearing new shoes. After twenty minutes of this one-way conversation that everyone in the carriage could hear, her friend chipped in. With an even louder voice she stood up, red in the face, and retorted: *"For God's sake, it's only a pair of shoes. I can't believe you keep saying you're so stressed. If you were in my situation you'd understand what stress really is. In less than three days I'm out of a job and right now there's no prospect of a new one. Stop friggin moaning."*

Clearly irritated, she got up and plonked herself three rows away in an empty seat.

You could have heard a pin drop. I wonder if you, like most people, believe that job loss stress is greater than the shoeless stress? Of course, I'd agree with you that the magnitude of the job loss seems greater, but in reality, how the body reacts - the hormonal and neurochemical responses in the brain - is exactly the same. This reaction is called *'fight or flight'* and to understand it, take yourself back to primal man before the world of computers, phones, TVs and shops. Primal man had to survive: he had to hunt, but similarly he could be the one hunted, so his body had an inbuilt system to help him respond to predators. He could either fight the predator or run away – fast!

That mechanism still exists within us today and in cases of emergency it is a perfectly normal reaction and serves us very well. The physical body responds to danger or threat immediately by alerting our hormones - the adrenal glands, the pituitary gland and the hypothalamus - to trigger defensive mechanisms such as raising our adrenaline and cortisol levels. The effect of this increases our heart rate, blood pressure and respiration. These symptoms are meant to stay active for just a few seconds or minutes, just long enough to help you fight or flee from the danger presented. But unfortunately, modern day life is so busy and stressful that many people are seldom out of fight or flight mode. You don't need a shoe incident or a job loss to induce the fight or flight response. You might simply find yourself perpetually stressed every day by your own exacting standards, or by trying to get somewhere on time, or by trying to meet deadlines and taking too much on. You may find this fight or flight occurs in your body when you imagine that you are going to be late or start thinking about all the things that might go wrong with your day; maybe an imagined confrontation with a colleague or an argument with a partner.

Everyone has an internal 'bath', a bath that is the measure of how much stress we can tolerate before it overflows. Provided that your bath is not full, new stressors can come into your life and you can deal with them adequately so that they don't affect you negatively. But if your bath starts to overflow as a result of constant fight or flight, something will inevitably break under the pressure, just like a weak link in a chain. The weak link will show up as a hormonal imbalance, energy fluctuations, mood swings, reduced immunity, burn out and physical or mental exhaustion.

Q. Did you know that 70 percent of your immune system is in your gut? How you feed your body affects your immunity.

Some stress is good for us. But the key is being able to recognise when your body is trying to tell you that your bath may be about to overflow.

The only thing is, right now, you might be so busy that you don't have time to have the consciousness. Perhaps you are so accustomed to your own coping strategies - getting on with doing it all, being on automatic pilot, enslavement, suppressing your real feelings - that your stress only starts to be in your awareness when everything starts to feel like you're running uphill in treacle. When everything starts to become a weighty effort it's still possible to keep going and keep coping, putting on the mask that says everything is fine, because saying anything else feels too weak or flaky. Anything else might reveal vulnerability, a vulnerability that says, *"I need help"* and, *"I can't keep all the balls spinning"*, a vulnerability that leads to feelings of guilt because you can't do it all. But by hiding behind this mask, a straw will arrive one day that might just break the camel's back.

> *"Stress is the cause of at least 95%*
> *of all illness and disease."*
> Dr Bruce Lipton ~ Cellular Biologist and Author
> 'The Biology of Belief'

The Girl With The Orange Hair

If you had been with me on one particular day, a Saturday a decade ago, you'd have seen that it was a bad hair day. In fact, it had been a bad hair day every day for the previous week. Every time I'd looked in the mirror, I'd been reminded of the fact that my colour needed doing and I needed a good cut. This Saturday I phoned my usual hairdresser and, of course, it being her busiest day, she was fully booked. My hair couldn't wait an hour longer so I turned up on spec at a recently opened salon close to where I lived. This new salon was glamorous: purple chaise lounges adorned the reception and opulent chandeliers hung from the ceiling. To my relief, they had a gap and could fit me in straight away. The hair technician (that's what they're called these days) was in his mid-twenties and was wearing the skinniest jeans I have ever seen on a bloke. *"What are we doing with your hair, Darling?"* he asked. My reply? *"Highlighted baby blonde please."*

Two hours later, after I'd read and reread several out of date copies of *Vogue*, he began the task of removing the foils - enough to wrap a dozen Christmas turkeys! And then he started to blow dry. I watched in the mirror - horrified. What was his definition of blonde? He had made me orange. Nothing wrong with orange, but not with my complexion!

Job done, he paraded around me with the handheld mirror, giving me glimpses of the sides and back while oohing and aahing. As he did so, I nodded compliantly and said, *"Yes that's lovely."* At the till, I parted with several twenty pound notes hoping and praying that the chandelier lighting in the salon was deceiving me. I ran to the car and checked in the rear view mirror...

It was still orange!

I was meeting my sister for lunch and drove the short distance to her house. She opened the door and gave me a look that said, *"What have you done to your hair?"*

Have you ever had one of those *'straw that breaks the camel's back'* moments? I found myself crying uncontrollably for about five minutes, and deep inside I knew I wasn't really crying for my hair. It was simply an emotional overwhelm, the culmination of everything that was going on in my life. The stress, my exacting standards of perfection for myself personally and professionally, the targets at work, my need to please everyone, the constant inner voice that criticised me for not being good enough, doing enough. My sister said, *"Its only hair, you can get it fixed."* In that moment, I thought, *"Liz, if you give yourself permission now you could have a nervous breakdown."* But a spilt second later, I had put the metaphorical coping mask back on, pulled myself together, stopped crying and said *"I'm OK."* I went to the bathroom, fixed my mascara and realised I could get my regular hairdresser to fix my disastrous do in a couple of days. Which of course I did.

With hindsight, I wonder whether I should have given in to how I was really feeling that day. Should I have taken off the mask and really examined my addiction to people pleasing and saying yes when I really meant no? Should I have examined my addiction to perfection and how I was constantly distracting myself from how I was feeling in my everyday life? If I'd taken my consciousness to the fact that mentally, emotionally and physically I felt exhausted, and given myself permission to be kinder to myself, then would I have ended up with cancer two years later?

That's an impossible question to answer.

But I wasn't a Warrior Woman then. I hadn't got the courage to reveal any vulnerability, admit any addictions or allow myself to truly feel. My coping mask of strength fronted it day in, day out.

At that time, I didn't realise that there is a miraculous healing system inside all of us that is capable of fixing any problems before they surface, but I'll talk about that later.

Q. Are you wearing the coping mask that externally fronts it? Are you trying to be strong because anything less than that seems weak or flaky? Are you suppressing an emotion? What if suppressing an emotion contained at a very cellular level, or a deep-seated stress, had the potential to reduce your immunity?

We all know about the immune system; its purpose is to repel pathogens: bacteria, virus, fungi and abnormal cells. I didn't realise then that prolonged and unaddressed stress, as well as suppressed emotion, has the capacity to reduce immunity, which in turn may make us more vulnerable to exhaustion, illness and disease.

Just how exactly stress affects the immune system has long been debated, but when I studied the relatively new field of *psychoneuroimmunology* (the study of how the mind can affect the immune system), it started to make sense to me. The word comes from the Latin roots *psych* (meaning mind), *neur* (meaning nerve or nervous system) and *immuno* (meaning immune), and if we can grasp that the body is more than just a collection of its parts and systems and open our minds to see it as a whole (holistically) then it makes sense that there is no division between the physical, mental and emotional body.

I want to make it clear here that I'm not saying that stress *equals* cancer. What I am saying is that an overload of your stress bath has the potential to *reduce immunity*, and that makes us more vulnerable to illness and disease. I am saying that hiding behind the coping mask of strength is denial: coping is not the same as healing. It takes courage to reveal vulnerability.

Watch Your Language

Once I had a consciousness of the healing power of nutritious food and how it played a role in promoting immunity, my newfound desire to eat well was a no-brainer. It was empowering and energising, and I couldn't fail to notice how much more vital I felt – even with the diagnosis. But the next part of my journey back to wellness was even more profound. When I developed a consciousness of how I could feed my mind, it was a total revelation. I realised how thoughts and words had the power to compound stress, reduce self-esteem and mentally paralyse me. When this became apparent, I was in a place of complete surprise and wonderment. Why didn't they teach this at school?

I was reminded of an audio I had heard some years previously. The presenter Peter Thomson (a UK leading strategist on business and personal growth) had revealed Earl Nightingale's (the Dean of Personal Development) little known secret: *"What you say will be the way."*

How you feed your mind, and speak your inner dialogue, is what you get.

> *"If you can't change it,*
> *change the way you think about it."*
> *Maya Angelou ~ Acclaimed Civil Rights Activist,*
> *Author and Poet*

Everything started to change for me on the day I realised that my thoughts, words and actions could play a part in my own wellness and affect how the rest of my life unfolded. I suddenly understood that I hadn't consciously invited two cancer diagnoses into my life, but when I saw how I could reprogram my mind for health, happiness and wealth, *my life turned around.*

But for me to understand this, I had to learn about my two minds. The conscious mind and the subconscious one. The conscious mind is the one that makes decisions for you about what to wear each day, which route to take to your appointment, what to have for dinner, and so on. Your conscious mind is also the one that allows you to learn new things, e.g. speak a new language or play an instrument. But surprisingly, your conscious mind represents no more than five percent of your total mind. The remainder is your subconscious and it is this part of the mind that many people would claim is in your heart. It is estimated that your subconscious mind has as many as 100,000 thoughts a day.

Q. How many times a day do you have the same habitual thoughts?

Your subconscious is the master controller of your life and has the capacity to restore homeostasis – a balance that can regulate your breathing, heartbeat, blood circulation, digestion and other bodily functions without you really being conscious of it. That's why it's called sub *(below)* conscious. Additionally, your subconscious holds all manner of learned and habitual behaviours. For example, when you first learned to write your name, you had to take your conscious awareness to it. Even though you were young you had to remember how to identify each letter and which followed which. Now you write your name automatically. You just do it without having to take your conscious awareness to it.

When you got older, you may also have learned to drive. You had to get to grips with how to coordinate the pedals with the gears, but now you've done it so often it has become a habit. You simply get in the car and get to your destination without having to consciously be aware of changing the gears, looking in your mirror or moving your feet. It's a learned behaviour, like a computer program that runs in the background on your human hard drive. It is below your consciousness.

From here on in, I'll refer to the subconscious as your *'program'*. It is the storehouse of your memory. Your program knows nothing about the concept of time; it only lives in the present. If you learned to swim 25 years ago, your program will not know if it was 10 years or 10 minutes ago – it just holds the memory of how to do it. Your program is subjective, it has no ability to think or rationalise independently like the conscious mind. It doesn't know the difference between right and wrong, good and bad, truth and lies or reality and imagination. It will not argue with you or answer back, it merely obeys the commands it receives from your conscious mind. It believes what you tell it. Liken your conscious mind to a gardener who is planting vegetable seeds. Your program becomes the garden in which the seeds germinate and grow. The conscious mind plants the seed and your program obeys by growing the vegetables. It is a faithful servant and it will not argue with you. Your program knows what to do - it's just that it doesn't know that it knows. It is also the seat of your emotion and perceives by intuition, or what you may call a sixth sense, inner trust, faith or belief. That belief is in your heart.

The words that you say out loud about yourself, as well as your inner talk, will be heard loud and clear by your program. If you say *"I can't"* or *"I'm no good"* or *"I'm a fat cow"* or *"it always happens to me"*, etc., your program will take you at your word. Your program cannot joke; it receives your planted message literally. If you look in the mirror and say to yourself how old, wrinkly, haggard, ugly, spotty or flabby you are, your program will always take you at your word because it has no power to rationalise what you are saying. It doesn't have the facility to contradict or disbelieve you.

Q. How often do you look in the mirror and say less than kind things to yourself?

The relatively new field of epigenetics reveals how the biological behaviour of the human cell is influenced by its environment. That means how the cell is fed with food and exposed to toxins, etc. But its environment also includes the subconscious – your program. Your cells are the garden that receives the seeds. The seeds will respond to the level of nurture you give them, and that includes the words you speak out loud and say with your inner voice. Consider the magnitude of this: if you say, *"breast cancer runs in my family, I'm bound to get it,"* your program might just accept this as a truth.

What if by changing your perception you could alter the fate of your cells? What if your mind had greater power than your genetic pre-disposition?

What if the very thing that has prevented you from getting all you want in life - wellness, love, happiness and abundance was not outside of you? How about if it was *already* inside of you? What if that thing inside was your subconscious program that's constantly talking to you?

But here's the thing. Nothing is likely to change until you have a consciousness of the program you are running and become aware of the level of self-nourishment you afford yourself with the *'seeds'* of food, kind thoughts and words.

Q. How much are you worth?

> *"Harnessing the power of your mind can be more effective than the drugs you have been programmed to believe you need."*
> Bruce Lipton PH.D. ~ *American cell biologist*

When I sussed this quote, *it was a revelation.*

How could it be that I had got to the age I had without realising the magnitude of this? I had so many habitual and less than kind thoughts about myself. The mind movies I continually replayed involved me questioning my capabilities, comparing myself to others and criticising myself. I'd lost count of the times I had played a mind movie of a bad day before I'd even got out of bed. And guess what? A bad day had followed. Or I'd replay a mind movie of something that had happened weeks ago, allowing myself to step back into feelings of resentment, blame, shame, humiliation, embarrassment, rejection, anger and guilt.

I'd mulled over those feelings again and again.

On my consciousness journey, I started having an awareness of my own language – both spoken and written. I looked at the many times I used the word should and imposed an expectation on myself. Well, I knew I was a people pleaser, most of us are – we all want to be liked and we are always seeking approval, recognition or a feeling of significance from others. That behaviour has been inbuilt from day one; from the day you wanted a smile from your Mummy or Daddy, or praise for using the potty.

Being a people pleaser meant I said yes too many times. I set myself unrealistic timescales then blamed my corporate world or felt resentful towards other people for sabotaging my time. I also started noticing that I said sorry far too many times for things that were not even my fault. I felt guilty for taking time to please myself.

Q. Do you do this? Do you apologise for things that are not your fault? Do you feel guilty if you take time for yourself?

It may be the case that right now you feel stuck or are resigned to a health/relationship/job or financial problem. Maybe you are unwittingly feeding yourself with less than useful words, non-serving inner dialogue and unhelpful mind movies? What if you are so unconscious of your program that it simply accepts your words and thoughts as truth?

The first step of the KindnessCODE is to develop a *consciousness* of the words you use.

Listen to how you may label situations as bad, hard, difficult, desperate, frightening, overwhelming, hopeless or worrying. If you have an illness, do you say: *"I am suffering from, battling against/or fighting with XYZ?"* Do you often say, *"I'm sensitive to or I need protection from?"* Do you find yourself saying *"sorry"* when it's not your fault, subconsciously putting yourself in a place of guilt for something you haven't even done wrong? If so, you might just be compounding your situation. It's called autosuggestion. Your words suggest to you the outcome. Let me emphasise that this isn't about covering up, hiding or being in denial about a situation, but there are different ways of reframing or viewing it. How about using the word *'challenge'* to describe a difficult situation, or *'recovering from'* instead of *'fighting against'*? These words have a less dense vibration and open the door to the possibility of a positive outcome.

You might want to take the time in your everyday life to tune into other people's language: colleagues, partners, parents, children and even people in the supermarket. Observe their body language and facial expressions. See how people unwittingly perpetuate stress and negativity in their life by the words they use, and how that language reflects in their physicality. Notice how they give their power away by blaming others.

How often do you hear these common statements?

"Things are desperate."

"It's frightening the way..."

"This is hopeless."

"Struggling on."

"I can't afford that."

"It's the government's fault."

> *"An entire sea of water cannot sink a ship.*
> *Similarly, the negativity of the world cannot put you*
> *down unless you allow it to."*
> *Anon*

You could also take your consciousness to the news, either on the radio or TV. Really listen to the words that are being used to describe the day's events. Pretty soon you will latch on to exactly what I mean. Broadcasters frequently use words such as: scarcity, lack, death, disease, insecurity, misery, suffering, disaster, hopelessness, struggle, failure, danger, blame, fight, revenge, pain, terror, grief, gloom and despair. Well, of course, it's the news, but these words have the capacity to perpetuate fear and stress, if we let them. I call these words dense words.

How often are words like these part of your everyday vocabulary? Once you take your consciousness to dense words, you will notice how they have the capacity to make your energy sink. Consider this: you may not willingly invite these words into your program, but even without paying attention to the news, they will still affect you at a very subliminal level, below your consciousness. It is called *heterosuggestion*. In other words, other people's words can shape your beliefs. They unconsciously become part of your program, add to your stress and confirm that the world is an unsafe place. It's a bit like being hypnotised with your eyes wide open.

Next, take your awareness to adverts. These can have the same effect. How frequently do you hear statements that subconsciously perpetuate fear? Adverts that say one in three people die of XYZ, or A is a risk factor for B? Imagine how disempowering statements like these could affect your health, joy and yes, even your wealth. Unless you consciously challenge the statement, your subconscious program will accept it. Remember, it is your willing servant - it has no potential to disbelieve what it is being fed. Once you have recognised this perhaps you, like me, will want to expose yourself to the news less and less, often because you will have the awareness of how the words used make you feel, and how they have an impact at a very subliminal level. Or, if you don't want to avoid the news and adverts, then ask yourself:

Is that really true for me?

Your program also has the capacity to play out your thoughts and beliefs in pictures and imagery that supports your spoken and inner talk. You have at your disposal a megastore of mind movies that can start playing as soon as you wake up. Before you have even got out of bed, your mind movie may be playing out an anticipated day of struggle and angst, maybe a disagreement with a colleague, a traffic jam, an accident, a missed plane, some threat, incident, danger or disaster. Do you get the picture? Most of the time this program is so below your consciousness that you are not even aware you are playing the movie. Your program also has the capacity to replay movies in your mind, reminding you of events that happened yesterday, last week, two years ago, and so on. It can replay them in pictures and words to remind you of times when you felt less good, less worthy, less significant, less attractive, less loved, less fulfilled. Incidents that made you feel ashamed, rejected, humiliated, embarrassed and guilty. But here's the thing, because your program has no concept of time, forward dated movies and past dated movies are all happening now. It doesn't know that these events are in the past or in your future.

Remember the girl with the shoe drama on the 5.20 train? She was perpetuating her own program of stress and discord by taking her mind movie to a situation that hadn't happened yet. She was already playing out the outcome: the bitchy remarks that Pippa and Sophie would make. As she played that movie, her body was responding as though it was happening now. She was already experiencing those feelings of humiliation, embarrassment, shame or rejection.

> *"Your cells are all creators and will create the exact pattern which you give them."*
> Charles Haanel ~ New Thought Author, Philosopher and Business Man

What if these feelings could unwittingly give us a victim mentality?

Victim Mentality

A victim mentality is the belief that we have no influence over how life happens to us or how we respond to it. Victim mentality happens at a very subliminal level. There is no judgment here, it's just that victim mentality people do not yet have the consciousness of how they are unwittingly contributing to the health issues, scarcity or discord in their life.

Victim mentality people run a mind program that typically says things like: *"Why me?"*/*"Oh, it always happens to me."* These are the people who say, *"Oh, it's alright for you because..."* Or they say, *"I never win."*/ *"I'll always be poor."* They might also remark, *"Ill health/obesity runs in my family."*/*"I haven't got a chance."*/*"What's the use, nobody cares."*/ *"I'm too old."*

These are the people that define themselves by their misfortune, and worry about stuff that hasn't even happened yet. They believe that bad luck is fate or ill health is inevitable. They see life as an endless grind and believe that their destiny is already fashioned by genes, education, locality, skin colour and other external factors.

These are the people who allow themselves to be hypnotised with their eyes wide open. They listen to the adverts that say one in three people... and their subconscious program accepts it. But it only believes it because they do not have the consciousness that they could be being fed an untruth. The message is so below their conscious awareness that they don't choose to ask the question – is this really true for me?

These are the people who find it easier to blame someone else for their lot in life. They are often jealous, sarcastic, bitchy or resentful of other people's good fortune. Often times, they are not even conscious that their cup is half empty; they moan a lot and can suck the energy out of everyone in their vicinity. They use dense words in their vocabulary all day, every day.

These are the people who light up the room when they leave it!

They give their power away by saying it someone else's fault.

Q. Do you know someone like this? We all do.

As I've said before, there is no judgement here. These were some of my traits until I learned about how to feed my mind and take my consciousness to the fact that I could claim some responsibility for my life.

The biggest lesson I learned from one of the first self-help books I read was to STOP being a VICTIM. At that time, the instruction felt very insulting. Here I was with my second cancer diagnosis – how could I not be a victim? But once I examined my consciousness and gained an awareness of how my words, thoughts and actions could have played a part in my situation, and, more significantly, how my new thoughts, words and actions could play a part in my wellness, everything changed. I took my consciousness *away* from my misfortune and moved it *to* my fortune - all the things I did have. I could still see, hear, walk, talk, write, drive, iron, type, and so on, and I felt gratitude for what I had in comparison to others who were less fortunate. My focus changed. I had a different perspective. All of a sudden, the things that I took for granted had a value, even the tedious things like ironing. I became grateful that I could iron - someone without arms would wish they could. Next, I took my consciousness to how I could feel and be in touch with my physical body. I made time to be with my physicality, noticing if my shoulders were hunched up by my ears, or if I was breathing quickly and shallowly from my lungs instead of my abdomen. I also took the time to be in touch with my emotions. How was I really feeling? I examined whether I was angry, sad, frustrated, or feeling rejected or humiliated, and so on. I allowed myself time to really feel my emotions and made a conscious effort to gaze at the clouds, even if it was only for a few minutes.

Once I had taken my consciousness to my spoken word and inner dialogue and realised that I had been speaking a victim mentality, *everything* changed.

> *"Until you stop breathing, there is more right with you than wrong with you."*
> Jon Kabat-Zinn, Founder of MBSR (Mindfulness-based Stress Reduction)

Are you focusing on the wrong things?

I recognised that I had perpetuated the stress in my corporate life by talking about it – a lot! My buzz words were stressed out/overwhelmed/drowning (in pressure)/not enough hours in the day. My job required visiting business clients so I was on the road quite a lot. For personal security reasons, we had an end of day policy to phone a designated colleague to confirm that we were safe. I used this phone time to generally moan about my struggle, the pressure I was under and how shit my day had been. (Sorry Sarah. It is OK for me to apologise here!)

Meanwhile, I discovered on my new journey of consciousness that the happiest and most fulfilled people see that life doesn't just happen. They know what they are seeking and they consciously become co-creators of their own life through their thoughts, inner dialogue, spoken word, vision and actions. They take responsibility for the great things that happen in their life, but here's the thing, they also take responsibility for the things that aren't so good. They are not in denial, but they understand that the less positive things are there to teach them something. They believe that everything happens for a reason. If we don't learn and grow from unpleasant experiences, we may unwittingly allow ourselves to step into victim mentality. If you are new to this concept, I don't underestimate how much of a challenge it may be to accept, but when you read the Warrior Women stories in this book, I'm sure it will make more sense.

Looking back, I believe my health challenges were simply a request from my heart/mind to be kinder to myself and develop self-nurture, self-compassion, self-worth and self-connection.

Q. Is your body in need of some self-kindness? Would you like to change your program?

At this point, you may want to buy yourself a nice journal to start recording some observations.

 Simply start by having *awareness – a consciousness*. Over the next few weeks, while you are at home, work and out and about, observe other people.

How often do they speak in dense words/sentences?

How normal is this language to them?

Do their facial expressions and general demeanour match their words? Do they look hunched up? Fidgety? Lopsided? Slouchy? Do they drag their feet, resist eye contact, or look defensive as though the world owes them something? Do they shrink into their body as though they are afraid?

Do you find that people respond negatively to positive statements? For example, if you make a general remark that the roads are clear, they'll reply that it will be murder as soon as the kids are back at school.

How do people respond when you ask them how they are? Are they average, not so bad or awesome?

Do they define themselves by their health, relationship (or lack of one) or their financial problems?

Do people try and invite you into their problem world?

Do you know people that cannot accept praise or compliments graciously?

Do they unwittingly wear a victim mentality?

Next, take *your* consciousness away from others and turn it on *yourself:*

Do you play that game of comparison? Do you have a pecking order determined by who has the biggest house, the best job, the biggest salary, the better car, the most intelligent kids, the slimmest waist and the most gorgeous wardrobe?

Are you trying to live up to someone else's expectations of you, or do you set unrealistic expectations for yourself?

Are you obsessed with trying to make everything perfect?

How do you respond when someone asks, *"How are you?"*

Notice how your physical energy feels.

How are you feeding and hydrating your body?

Do you sit and stand upright, or do you slouch? What is your demeanour like?

Do you feel comfortable with your physicality? Does it make you feel less or more?

Start to be the observer of your thoughts. Notice how many times you have the same habitual thoughts over and over. Is there a pattern or a theme with the feelings that these thoughts provoke?

Do you say yes when you mean no? Do you have trouble asserting yourself? Do you give an answer based on the path of least resistance? Perhaps one that you think will prevent confrontation? Are you a people pleaser?

Would you sooner give in or not try than risk the shame of failure?

Do you mentally label certain foods good and bad? Are you aware of how that makes you feel when you eat them?

Do you focus more on what is wrong with your life than what is right?

Examine your addiction, habit, compulsion or enslavement. Ask yourself: *is this addiction serving me? Are you in denial over anything?*

Can you get things into perspective? The news gives us grim stories but there are billions of people in the world, most of whom are having a pretty good time! They are not being shot, murdered, raped, robbed and terrorised, and they are not falling ill with incurable diseases.

How easy is it for you to take off your mask of strength? Would you feel vulnerable if you admitted how you really felt?

How guilty do you feel about putting your oxygen mask on first - metaphorically speaking? Can you put your own needs first?

Coping is not healing.

 PART TWO

Opportunity

*So, now you understand that everything starts with consciousness, let me introduce you to Part Two of the **KindnessCODE**; the letter **O**, which stands for **opportunity.***

When you seize this, everything in your life starts to become more aligned and more balanced.

Opening The Door To Opportunity

If you don't grasp the concept of opportunity,
nothing will ever change.

In my corporate life, I disliked the word opportunity; it was often used in the context of the following well-known phrase: *"We don't have problems, we only have opportunities."* The meaning behind this phrase is that we should turn a negative situation into a positive one, but it used to grate on me because it implied that problems should be denied, and of course we have problems. The opportunity as a Warrior is to not be in denial of a problem - it's to hold your hand up and have the courage to admit that there is one.

Your problem may be your addiction - your habit, your compulsion or enslavement - and once you have the courage to admit it, you can open the door to an opportunity of choice. Your choice is to reframe it, see it differently, give it new perspective or change the way you respond to it. Choice requires more than just being conscious of your addiction and positive of a new outcome. It requires action.

Sitting On The Nail

Have you ever joined in the countdown on New Year's Eve and wondered if the following 12 months were going to be '*your year*'? On January 1, you sensed a renewed promise of expectancy, but five days on, everything seemed exactly the same as last year. You found yourself stuck back in the groove. Same old, same old.

Or maybe you have had that feeling of being uncomfortably comfortable. You know you need to change but the nagging feeling this brings is more comfortable than the discomfort of doing something new.

I once heard this analogy:

Imagine likening your life to sitting on an old sofa - one that you've had for a lifetime. It is so knackered that the nails that hold the upholstery together have started to stick through. Every day you sit on this sofa, knowing that it is getting less and less comfortable, but you don't do anything about it until one day a nail impales your bum. Ouch! This nail is the only thing that makes you take some action. At last you make a choice whether to get off it, sit on another chair or buy another sofa.

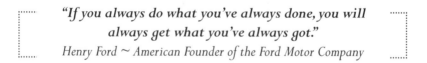

"If you always do what you've always done, you will always get what you've always got."
Henry Ford ~ American Founder of the Ford Motor Company

If you recognised from Part One that you have an addiction, compulsion, habit or enslavement then well done! But if you have chosen not to take your consciousness to it, it's possible that you are simply wearing the mask. It feels more comfortable to remain emotionally and mentally cut off and avoid facing the discord in your life. Wearing this mask over a prolonged period of time may start to make you feel out of ease with your inner self. You might have a sense of incongruence – you feel less and less authentic and out of touch with whom you really are. All of this can turn into mental and emotional stress until the time comes when the straw breaks the camel's back or the nail sticks in your bum. Please don't wait until the discord in your life manifests physically or mentally as a physical illness, nervous exhaustion or depression/anxiety. And definitely don't wait until it becomes illness or dis-ease.

> *Opportunityisnowhere*
> *Q.What do you read here?*
> *"Opportunity is nowhere" or "Opportunity is now here?"*

Before God's velvet hammer came and banged me on the head for the second time, deep down I knew I felt uneasy. I felt stuck in my corporate world and although I had a desire to do something different, this prospect was just too daunting. Although my job wasn't a typical desk job and gave me a fair amount of variety, I was uncomfortably comfortable. I had done it for years and I knew it inside out. It paid for my lifestyle but it left me stale and my energy was stagnant. It was beyond me to even believe I could put myself out there and risk rejection. (I will explain more about fear, loss and rejection in Part Four.) I didn't have the courage to put my hand up and admit that there was a discord. Every year I would think, *"next year will be different"*. But come mid-January, it was same old, same old.

Perhaps you are aware of wanting something different in your life. Maybe you want to achieve your ideal weight, improve your health, have more energy, take up a new hobby, end an abusive relationship, gain more respect from your partner or work colleagues or set up your own business. However, you recognise that this requires some change. It may be that your interpretation of change conjures up huge feelings of fear and anxiety. Maybe you think it requires massive amounts of willpower, effort, discipline and strength. Or maybe you believe that it involves the suppression or loss of something. So here's the thing - amend the word willpower to why power. Everything changes when you discover your 'why', and changing won't require willpower. Let me explain.

Why Power

I spoke before about your subconscious program. This holds your belief patterns, your long-term memory and your values. When you understand that your program is just a series of beliefs that have fashioned your behaviour, everything starts to slot into place. Most of your beliefs and values will have stemmed from situations and events in your life that happened before the age of seven. These beliefs have been passed down from other people (family, teachers, friends, etc) through heterosuggestion. As I mentioned before, they will also have been passed down on a subliminal level via the media. Yes, even before the age of seven the TV and radio will have played a part in moulding your beliefs.

Once you take your consciousness to your program and start being the observer of your thoughts as well as the thinker of them, you may see that you are carrying round a huge storehouse of negative thoughts and feelings about yourself. These beliefs have made you feel less adequate, less talented, less attractive and less good. Once you have the conscious origin of these beliefs, you can start to see how they may have influenced your experience of life to date. You will also see how easy it would be to slip into victim behaviour. As soon as you have the consciousness of the program you are running, it becomes much more clear why stuff happens to you, why people behave the way they do with you and why you behave/react the way you do. You will be able to see how this may have blocked you from making changes or stopped you from seeing your own magnificence. You may also see how you have perpetuated these beliefs through autosuggestion – your inner voice speaking to you. That is, how you have unwittingly reduced your own self-worth by using less kind words to describe yourself in your head and out loud, which may have led to you sabotaging your own endeavours. You may see that the only reason you have an addiction – habit, compulsion or enslavement - is because you are trying to fill a gap that distracts you from your own feelings of not being good or worthy enough.

But here's the thing. Don't blame yourself. It's not your fault. Once you can see how these beliefs no longer serve you, you can then change your program.

We attract what we believe. Until we control our beliefs, they control us.

As you start to think more about your words and beliefs, it's possible that you will see an emerging pattern of events that have compounded your thoughts of feeling less throughout your life. In my *'Discover Your Why and Worth'* seminars/retreats, I often use the table-top analogy.

Visualise a table-top. You are the table-top. The first time that you felt ashamed or humiliated - let's say someone in the school playground picked on you or mocked you - your table-top grew a leg. The next time you felt this way was when the teacher announced in front of the whole class that you couldn't sing and asked you to leave the choir. At this moment your table-top grew another leg. The headmaster identified someone in your school as the *'best'* and by default that made you feel less than best. You got called a loser – another leg appeared. Let's say you got bullied because you didn't fit in: perhaps you looked different or didn't conform to the rest of the gang – another leg appeared. Then, as you got older, other stuff happened. Your first boyfriend chucked you, you were ostracised from a group or failed your exams. All of this made you feel less good, less adequate, less talented, less competent, less capable, less attractive, less clever and less gifted. And every time another event like this happened, the more it reinforced your beliefs, and the more the legs from your table-top grew. Before you knew it, you had got to your middle years with more legs supporting the table-top than you could shake a stick at!

The feelings attached to these legs had become so deeply imprinted that they moved you further and further away from an acceptance of yourself, so much so that it feels normal to not feel good about yourself. The way you think others see you and how you see yourself is not very complimentary. You might punish yourself with less than kind words, self-harm, too many comfort foods or drink and drugs.

Your feelings of being less have removed any compassion for yourself because you are continually playing a program that reinforces your belief that you are less than worthy. You feel insignificant, no longer worthy of putting your oxygen mask on first.

If your why is big enough, you won't need will power.

Once you have the consciousness that your program is merely a series of beliefs that made you behave in a certain way, you can find enough reasons why change has to happen and make some new choices.

In Part One, I suggested that you take your consciousness to your body as well as to the words you hear and say. Now let's take your consciousness to your beliefs. When you are conscious of the program that's running on your internal hard drive, you can take the opportunity to change it.

Examine your beliefs around:

→ Your self-esteem, confidence and ability to do or achieve something new.

Do you focus on doubt, worry and/or other people's judgement? Do you experience feelings of shame, humiliation or rejection if you don't succeed?

→ Your perception of time.

Do you feel annoyed, irritated, disappointed or even sad that other people rob you of your time? Does it feel like time is getting faster or running out?

→ Relationships, love and respect. (This may involve a partner, family, friends and colleagues.)

Do you feel taken for granted, unappreciated or rejected? Or do you feel betrayed or abused physically, mentally or emotionally?

→ Health, wellness and body image

What do you believe about your physicality, genetics and ageing? Do you believe you can play a part in how well you feel and look?

→ Security, money and abundance.

Every time you hear the post drop through the letterbox and land on the mat, do you declare: *"Oh no, more bills?"* Do you pay your bills grudgingly? Are you aghast at the total that pings up on the till when you are in the supermarket, and do you hand over your payment while tut-tutting inside? Do you focus on scarcity and lack, only noticing what you don't have or can't afford?

Some weeks ago, when I was at the hairdressers (again!), my hairdresser, a gorgeous Asian woman in her 30s, asked me the polite question: *"How are you?"* I replied by saying, *"Thanks for asking, I'm great."* But when I asked her the same question she said reservedly, *"I'm OK"*. I couldn't help but ask her why she was only OK. Straight away she said, *"I only ever say I'm OK because if I say I'm anything more then that's like tempting fate and something bad might happen."*

I was puzzled, but the more we spoke, the more it became evident that her program had imprinted at a very early age. Two questions she remembered her parents asking her a lot in her childhood were: *"Who do you think you are? What makes you think you are so great?"*

She had grown up with a belief that it *wasn't right* to be great.

Q. Ask yourself this. What is wrong with being great? (That doesn't translate as arrogant, conceited or vain, rather it means stepping into the magnificence of who you are.)

Your beliefs form your reality because every belief carries an emotion. It is the emotion behind the belief that magnetically attracts. So, if you believe you are unattractive, unworthy or poverty stricken then others will see you this way, too. Like attracts like. If these are your beliefs then other people are unlikely to compliment or praise you, and they . will probably walk all over you instead.

Once you have examined the origin of your table-leg beliefs then you can challenge the truth of them in the same way that you would dispute the TV advertisement that states: One in three people are at risk of XYZ.

Examine your beliefs. Ask yourself: *Is this really true for me? Where is the evidence to support it?*

I share the *RED lipstick technique* with the women I work with. When you hear a disempowering statement or notice that you are thinking a non-serving thought, take out an imaginary red lipstick and draw a big red cross through it. Replace it with something more empowering.

New T&Cs

Give yourself the opportunity to be conscious of what you are inviting into your life physically, mentally and emotionally. Examine where the beliefs that you are not good enough have stemmed from.

Know that any addiction you have is not wrong; it is simply a program – a table leg (or several) that has endorsed a belief that you are worth less.

Set some new **T&Cs** for yourself. These are new standards or rules that will help you live life more on *your* terms. Make a kindness contract with yourself.

 In your journal, write out some promises to be kinder to yourself.

Everything started to change for me on the day I realised, metaphorically speaking, that I had been sitting on the nail. The magnitude of my health challenges gave me the chance to get a different perspective on the health I already had, and what was important in my life. I saw an opportunity to challenge my beliefs, say yes to life and play an active part in being well, happy and fulfilled. I gave myself permission to value my time, which involved saying *"no"* to other people's demands if I chose. Saying *"no"* became a conscious choice that I was saying *"yes"* to myself. I let go of the guilt.

Q. Could you give yourself permission to start saying "no" in order to say "yes" to yourself? Could you let go of the guilt attached to putting your oxygen mask on first?

I gave myself the opportunity to observe my spoken and written words, and removed the word sorry when it wasn't my fault. I set new realistic timescales for myself that gave me breathing space. I stopped making promises to people that put me under undue pressure. And a big one - I gave up my need for everything to be perfect, both at home and professionally. Instead, I gave myself permission to acknowledge more of the things that were right with me. I looked at all my achievements rather than focusing on the things I hadn't done and didn't like about myself. I started thanking my body for all that it did for me. I stopped blaming other people for my lot in life and realised that it was up to me to take responsibility. I gave myself permission and courage to take off the mask that was hiding how I really felt and who I really was. I no longer sought a sense of identity from the title on my business card.

The potentiality of your life from now on starts with you being willing to change your program. But just in case you haven't already realised it, that means your oxygen mask must go on first. It's not greedy or selfish. When you put your oxygen mask on first you can start making a real difference to others. You are no use to anyone if you can't breathe.

Imagine that from now on, your perspective on life, and the level of appreciation and respect you get from others, is directly proportional to the level of self-kindness you afford yourself.

So here's the thing. If you believe that you are worth the change then the rest is easy. You probably won't need to read the rest of this book. But if there is a nagging doubt here then we need to address some deep-seated beliefs that you hold about your own self-worth. We need to look at what you really believe about yourself and the life you deserve.

Before we look at beliefs some more, you may be sensing that you need to get off the nail, only the magnitude of the leap just seems too big. So here's the story of Lynda's Masterpiece to show you it doesn't need to be this way.

Lynda's Masterpiece

Lynda had taken early retirement, and with some extra time on her hands took a bold step and joined a local art class. Secretly, she had always harboured a desire to draw and paint, but she'd not done anything since her school days. The art class was open all day every Wednesday for students to turn up as and when they pleased. The round faced, smiley teacher had an excellent reputation for helping people unleash their creativity and Lynda was given a warm welcome by the rest of the group. In her first few lessons, she was taught the basics of still art. How to see everyday objects – flowers in a vase, a teapot, cups and a chair – with a new perspective. Each object fitted into a shape: a circle, triangle, square or rectangle, so that Lynda could draw the object to scale. She loved what she was being taught and started to really look forward to her classes. Outside of them, she started to see everyday objects differently. Did they fit into a square, circle, triangle or rectangle?

Some weeks into the course, the teacher suggested to the students that they could paint a house with a garden. This was not going to be still art, this involved pure imagination and creativity. Lynda got to work. She started with a pencil outline and gradually filled it in with colour. The house was Victorian in style, with a front door at its centre and symmetrical windows on the ground and upper floors. It had dark red brickwork and a pitched roof. The green lawn of the garden curved in front of the house like a lush carpet.

From time to time, the teacher would stand behind Lynda observing her progress, nodding and declaring *"Mmmm"* enthusiastically. Lynda felt proud that her painting was coming together just as she had envisioned it. She was so engrossed that the time flew by and before she knew it, the class was coming to an end. As she packed away her paints, the teacher took one last glance at Lynda's effort and said, *"That's a good start, Lynda, but in next week's lesson think about how you might brighten it up a bit."* Lynda grimaced and felt flat inside. This was the best thing she'd ever done.

Indignant, she packed the painting into her portfolio carrier along with her brushes. Once home, still feeling deflated, she got to work on her masterpiece again. Painstakingly, she painted over every single red brick to reveal a new, white worn stucco exterior. It was tedious and time consuming, and it was almost midnight by the time she finished.

The following week, Lynda proudly pulled the painting from her portfolio carrier and awaited praise for her bright new creation. Perplexed, the teacher asked:

"Why did you change the brickwork?"

"You said make it brighter," Lynda replied.

"Oh, Lynda, what I meant was, how about putting some flowers in the garden? Some extra colour would make a huge difference to the beauty of your painting."

The point of this story is that sometimes assumed change is painstakingly huge and requires a big effort. However, in fact, the change required might be as simple as seeing things with a different perspective: the whole house doesn't need repainting but a small amount of colour wouldn't go amiss. Rome wasn't built in a day and baby steps add up. Set some new T&Cs that are relatively easy and enjoyable to adopt. In the fullness of time, these will add up to big change.

It reminds me of the following joke:

Q. How do you eat an elephant?
A. One bite at a time!

The SELF Principle

I believe that most decent human beings want to live a life that makes a difference to others. We want to feel that we have made a contribution in some way to man or womankind. It doesn't have to be a contribution of epic proportions, like being Mother Teresa or winning a Nobel Peace Prize, it may simply mean bringing up your kids well, being a good partner, doing your job to the best of your capabilities, sharing your gift or talent or being part of a community for change. If someone was reading your eulogy, I believe you would want to hear the words that your life held purpose. I call it the **SELF Principle.**

★ **S** stands for **SIGNIFICANCE**

Everyone wants to be recognised, have their name remembered or be made to feel special in some way. This started when you were a child and you got used to hearing your parents saying your name. You got told you were a "good girl" when you used the potty for the first time and got a pat on the back when you won your sports day or passed your spelling test. The word 'significance' may conjure up the image of a vain, self-important type, but that's not the type of person I am referring to. I simply mean that everyone has a desire to be seen and heard. Of course, we all like compliments and praise, but you also have to see and hear your own worth and your own uniqueness. You have to believe that you are already good enough to deserve whatever it is in life that you desire. Don't rely on getting your significance from others. Believe it is already within you.

★ **E** stands for **EMOTION**

Everything is a feeling. All feelings are emotions of some sort. We all want to feel the emotions of love and fulfilment.

★ **L** stands for **LOVE**

Everyone wants to feel loved, and it doesn't matter whether that is the love of a partner, child, friend or a pet. We all want to give and receive love and feel connected. The need for connection and belonging is a basic instinct. But receiving love from others always starts with the amount of love we show for ourselves. Again, this isn't a vanity thing. The interpretation of your life is how you value yourself and your time. The more time you spend with love and belief in yourself, the more love you will be able to share with others, and the more love will flow back to you.

★ **F** stands for **FULFILMENT**

We all want to feel that we have grasped the potentiality of life and achieved our hopes and desires. We are happy and satisfied when we have done something worthwhile. It feels like our cup is running over. We know that life has meaning and purpose, and that we are here on Earth for a reason. I believe that fulfilment comes when we truly love ourselves and are willing to step into our own magnificence and help others to do the same. When we do this we can leave a legacy. We can raise the vibration of everyone on this planet and help them to see that they are deserving of life's riches.

Q. How good would it feel to know that by affording yourself a higher level contribution of self-kindness, self-nurture, self-worth and self-connection, you could make a greater contribution to others?

You may want to record your answer to this question, and the next ones, in your journal.

 How can you open the door of opportunity? What small steps and new choices can you make to be kinder yourself?

Suggestions include:

- ✓ When showering, take your awareness and feel the sensation of the water caressing your skin. Wash yourself with tenderness and appreciation for your body.

- ✓ Get more perspective on your life. Stop sweating the small stuff. Ask yourself whether the problem you have today will really matter in five days, five months or five years' time.

- ✓ Take time to really see the flowers and the trees, and to really listen to the birds. Don't be in so much of a rush that you miss the beauty of everything.

- ✓ Give yourself permission to take a proper lunch break.

- ✓ Eat regularly. Missing meals will not give your body the fuel it needs to keep going. It will slow down your metabolism, potentially encouraging weight gain, and make you feel sluggish.

- ✓ Eat consciously. Take time to really taste and savour your food. Chew your food well before swallowing. Your digestion will thank you for it.

- ✓ Lose your attachment to good and bad. If you mentally label foods 'good' or 'bad' it's possible that you're putting yourself in a place of mental torture. Lose the labels. Nothing is good, nothing is bad- it's just that some things are better.

✓ Give a new meaning to the word urgent. Allow it to only represent the emergency services – saving a life. Anything else is not urgent!

✓ How tightly are you holding on? Feel the tenseness in your hands and let go. Loosen your grip on the steering wheel, your mouse, pen or the vegetable knife.

✓ Stop saying sorry if it's not your fault.

✓ Consciously hear the words and thoughts you have. Ask yourself, is this really true for me? What would I really choose? If the words are not empowering, apply the RED lipstick technique.

✓ Take time to stand still, really still. When you put the kettle on, allow yourself those few minutes to simply be with your breath and your heartbeat. NB, this is really kind.

PART THREE
Dreams & Desires

*You have now mastered your **C consciousness**, and understand how your thoughts, words and beliefs may have played a part in your life. You have also seized the **O opportunity** to make new choices. You see that significance, love and fulfilment are an inside job. Now let's move on to Part Three.*

*The **D** in the **KindnessCODE** stands for **Dreams** and **Desires**.*

*The **D** also stands for **Deserve**. You will only manifest the dreams and desires of your life if you have changed your program and adopted a new belief that confirms you deserve it.*

Daring To Dream

What do you desire in life?

What did you want to be when you grew up? When I was little, I wanted to be a hairdresser. My neighbour, auntie Sandra (everybody was an aunt or uncle in those days), was a hairdresser. She worked from home and I thought her life was fabulous. There was always a flow of folk in her house: people dropping by for a hairdo, coffee or a natter. She kept a plastic container on the kitchen work surface filled with a myriad of nail varnishes. I longed to be grown up enough to wear exotic nail colours.

That was when I was about eight or nine.

When I was in senior school that dream changed. I was averagely academic but I loved my art classes.

We had an outrageously unconventional teacher. She was half French and had wild, bright orange corkscrew hair. She wore ruby red lipstick and her clothes were mainly crushed velvet, usually in bold pink or purple, which, with her orange hair, was an unusual combination. Her nails were always varnished either vibrant pink or electric blue. She was different to all the other teachers at my school. They were much more conservative in their dress as well as their approach to teaching. The art lessons didn't even feel like being at school and they gave us the opportunity to be creative and produce something that could be admired. Our art teacher never judged our work as good or bad; it just was. I loved drawing. It helped me get into *'the flow'* and lose myself in the concentration of trying to create a finished piece. I used to dream that I could one day do this for a living. I would leave school and go to art college to master the art of painting and drawing.

When I got to 15, my parents sat me down for a talk and convinced me that a career in art wasn't a wise choice. *"Nobody makes a living from art,"* they said. *"Best look for a job that will give you some stability."* That is where my dream ended. There is no judgement here because my very alternative career taught me something very profound. I say 'alternative' because working for a bank was never on my radar. It was as far away from being an artist as I could imagine. My perception was that it was stuffy and conventional.

The small advertisement, cut out from the Birmingham Evening Mail, had been placed strategically on the lounge mantelpiece by my mother. *'Cashier wanted'*, it read. Mum suggested that I phone the next day and apply. Some days later, having been granted an interview, I showed up for the appointment. Sitting in the banking hall waiting to be called through was as far away from my dream as I could imagine, but when my name was called I jumped up. I followed the clerk through the door marked 'staff only' into the manager's office. From behind his huge desk he asked me dozens of questions and I found myself giving all the right answers. After 30 minutes that was that. He made it clear. Unless the next best thing to sliced bread walked through his office, I'd got the job. I knew my parents would be pleased but I didn't know whether to laugh or cry. I ended up working for the bank for a very long time. I became uncomfortably comfortable.

I'd still be there now if I hadn't discovered my *'why'*, but my why only became evident the day I started seeking answers to the challenge that I now refer to as God's velvet hammer, which had come and banged me on the head a second time. This hammer prompted me to make conscious kinder choices for myself. Then SELF-kindness (significance and the emotions of love and fulfilment), became my why. It became *my purpose.*

But I believe that I was meant to follow a banking career for a while. Why? What did it teach me? Well, in its simplicity, banking is all about investment and lending. People pay money in and the bank lends that money out in order to get a return on investment. If they lend out more than they have got in investments they go bankrupt. Let me explain before you tune out...

ROI Return On Investment

I mentioned before that you were born with two hands, symbolised as giving and receiving. Call them left for lending out or giving and right for investing or receiving. What is the relevance? When we give of ourselves - lend ourselves out disproportionately to the amount of kindness we allow ourselves to receive - life gets out of balance. This happens when we find ourselves saying yes when we really mean no. This makes us feel resentful. We feel as though our time is being manipulated. It builds up a huge frustration because there is no return on our investment. There is no return to the SELF. We start to feel less significant and we find it challenging to feel both love for ourselves or any fulfilment in our life. Really, we are sabotaging our own significance, love and fulfilment because when all is said and done, there is only time. Time is just a series of days, months and years that make up your life. Choose how you spend your time wisely. Make sure you invest in *you. You matter!* Your SELF kindness.

Nurture your body, feed your mind kindly and connect with the truth of who you really are.

What has this got to do with dreams?

Regardless of your age, have you ever dared to dream? Daydream, that is. Most people will say that they dream of winning the lottery. But the reality is they don't dream it. They just say it and wish it. That is not the same as really dreaming it.

Daydreaming requires playing a movie in your mind. Kids are expert at it. I love to watch my neighbour's four-year-old grandson acting out his make believe world of fictional characters and animals. He talks the movie out loud with no inhibitions. You'll have seen this yourself. Daydreaming was never a problem for you until you grew older and became self-conscious and worried that you were imagining stuff that wasn't really there.

So I wonder, have you ever allowed yourself to daydream about your most wanted car, a rewarding job, a better house, a fatter bank account, the partner of your dreams? Have you daydreamed about an exotic holiday or sharing the stage with someone famous? What about being on the Oprah show, winning a coveted award, writing a bestseller, directing a film, hearing your music played on the radio or seeing your work revered in a prestigious gallery? Have you dreamed that people are queuing up for your designs, expertise, product or service and thanking you for making a difference in their life? If you have had a daydream like this congratulations, but I wouldn't mind betting that you have also heard your little voice kick in. You know the one, the one that says, *"Don't be ridiculous, that will never happen."* Or, *"You can't do that, you are too old/too young/too unattractive/not rich enough/not clever enough/it won't happen in a million years."* If you have heard that little voice, and I'm sure you have, that will be your program. It's your subconscious mind trying to sabotage your dream. Or maybe you heard someone else's voice less than kindly sabotaging your dream for you?

Everything changed for me the day I realised that I'd spent the first half of my life being a passive participant in it. I'd allowed life to simply happen to me. I also realised that I didn't have a dream. Shock horror! At that moment, I decided to have one and, most significantly, I realised that I deserved it.

Money – what do you think about it?

In my one:2:one consultations with women, I always suggest we look at beliefs around money. You might ask why. Well, your relationship with money will usually be a reflection of your own self-worth and the bigger picture of whether you think you deserve wellness, joy and abundance. It is usually very revealing. What has money got to do with health and happiness?

> *"It's not possible to live a really complete and fulfilled life unless you are rich. You must have money to advance yourself and others."*
> The Right to be Rich, Wallace D Wattles ~ New Thought and Pioneer Success Writer

Q. What do you think about this statement?

You may have something in your program that says it's not true or doesn't feel right.

You may be thinking that money doesn't buy happiness. And I wouldn't disagree, so let me be clear here that this isn't about making money your prime focus in life to the exclusion of everything else. However, I do want you to understand that money is OK – well, pretty good actually. People might say it's not spiritual to be rich but that's because many of us grew up thinking there is something less good about money or that money was scarce.

 Have a think about which of the following sayings, associations or beliefs you grew up with around the words *'money'*, *'rich'* or *'wealthy'*. Write them down in your journal.

→ Money doesn't grow on trees.

→ Rich people are crooks.

→ Filthy rich.

→ Money is the root of all evil.

→ The rich get richer and the poor get poorer.

→ You only get money by working really hard.

→ It's selfish to want a lot of money.

→ Money doesn't equal happiness.

→ Money is not that important, it's only money.

→ Money is dirty.

→ Making loads of money is not spiritual.

Q. Do you avoid talking about money?

As you were growing up, what was your parents' attitude to money? Did they fight over it? Did you often hear them say *"we can't afford it"* or did you sense that there was never quite enough to go round and that life was all about penny pinching? What was their opinion of wealthy people? Did your parents celebrate other peoples' wealth or were they resentful or jealous?

Q. As you grew up, what was your own perception of people with money? If you had money, how did people react to you?

When I ask women the question, *"do you deserve to make the most of yourself, live life fully and feel totally fulfilled in the bargain?"* most will usually answer *"yes"*.

When I ask the same person *"do you deserve to be wealthy?"* most women are very hesitant to say yes and some answer no straight away. But here is the paradox: to make the most of yourself you will inevitably need money to do it.

If you find yourself thinking that this feels wrong, or it feels arrogant to say you deserve to be wealthy, then this is because your program has still got table legs, and these support your belief that you are worth less.

Q. If you could, would you choose to change your program and collapse the table legs that have made you feel less than worthy?

Once again, let me remind you that this isn't about making money your prime focus in life, but it is about understanding that money is OK. I'm simply using this comparison as a barometer of your self-worth.

Right now, don't concern yourself with any questions about how you might change, just tick the following statements that apply to you, if any.

I would like:

- ✓ More physical energy and stamina.
- ✓ To look and feel better, slimmer, healthier and sexier.
- ✓ More time feeling relaxed and in control of life.
- ✓ To change my job, pursue a business idea, follow my passion and get my 'thing' out there.
- ✓ To have more variety or adventure in my life.
- ✓ To have a new place to live or an additional place to live.
- ✓ To have more confidence in myself and accept myself.
- ✓ To overcome a wellness challenge.
- ✓ To have a relationship with someone that loves and respects me.
- ✓ To find a new identity now that my kids have flown the nest/my divorce is final/I've overcome my grief or another life-changing situation.
- ✓ To feel significant, valued and appreciated.
- ✓ To have financial freedom to enjoy all the things I love doing.
- ✓ To be paid my worth.

Looking at the statements you have ticked, ask yourself why do you want them? What will you gain by having them? Write your answers down in your journal. Spend some time doing this; it will really help prioritise what is important to you.

Now select the top three and write down your answers to the following questions:

➜ If I achieved this now, how would it make me feel?

➜ If I achieved this now, who would I become?

➜ If this is my real desire what will I lose by getting it or what will I have to lose by getting it?

The answers will reveal your inner beliefs – the table legs that remain your program, are blocking you from having whatever it is you desire and are subconsciously making you feel less in some way: less adequate, less attractive, less talented and less worthy. This program is running on your human hard drive and has the potential to affect your wellness, happiness and abundance.

Lucy

Lucy came to see me because of problems with her weight. She constantly ate foods that were adding to her waistline, hips and thighs. She had ballooned and admitted that she was five stone overweight. With two demanding young kids, her size meant that she had less energy to devote to them. She described herself as a fat slob. Every time she looked in the mirror she had feelings of self-loathing and said, *"I hate you, Lucy,"* but nevertheless, she couldn't stop eating. Her mind was obsessed with doubts about how long her husband would remain with her looking like she did. Lucy adored fashion but buying clothes for her size had become a nightmare. Whenever there was a family get together, her weight would be the topic of conversation: everyone seemed to have an opinion on her eating habits and how they could improve. She was fed up of listening to it and wanted to tell them all where they could get off.

When Lucy came to see me it was evident I didn't need to educate her on food. She knew precisely which foods she could be eating more of, and those she should avoid. Lucy admitted that she was fully aware that she was slowly killing herself. This was a significant confession.

She then told me that she had attempted suicide when she was a student.

Growing up hadn't been easy for Lucy. Her mother had brought her and her three siblings up single-handed in very tough conditions. She worked full time in a lowly paid job and juggled work with domestic responsibilities. She desperately tried to keep a roof over their heads, pay the bills, clothe them and put food on the table, but inevitably there were days when they went without. It seemed like there was never enough to go around. When Lucy and her siblings grew older and flew the nest, her mother threw herself into her work, securing better and better positions. She worked her way up the career ladder and some 15 years on, had an enviable job and all the perks that went with it. She won countless awards and accolades for her work along the way; her achievements were awesome.

Lucy was full of admiration for her mother and looked up to her. She had gone from 'nothing', in her words, to being top of her profession. Her mother was on a pedestal. Even though Lucy was 35, she still sought her mother's opinion on just about everything. She couldn't trust her own decisions and needed constant validation that she was making the right choices. The more Lucy spoke, the more it became evident that she revered her mother so much that it was a huge challenge for her to believe that she could live up to how great her mother had become. The woman who had raised her and her sisters single-handed, now had executive responsibility and a handsome salary.

I asked Lucy why she had wanted to kill herself. This unravelled a deep-seated belief that she would never be able to match up to her mother's achievements. But in the same breath, Lucy said that it felt wrong to even think that she could try to be as good as her mother. If she did, she would feel guilty; she could never overshadow the light that shone on her mother.

While she remained overweight and looking the way she did, she could remain less against her mother's greatness. Overeating meant that she would never have to step into the magnificence of who she was. She wouldn't even have to try to shine her own light for fear that she might not be good enough. She could play 'small' against her mother's reputation. It was a protection for her. Her overeating was a habit that meant she didn't have to risk feeling ashamed or humiliated if she failed.

I asked Lucy what she would lose (apart from pounds and stones) by achieving her ideal weight. She thought it was a strange question but her answer was revealing. She pondered a while and replied that if she lost weight she felt sure that she would lose friends. She'd never thought about it consciously, but losing weight had the potential to lose her the love of her friends, the ones that had always sympathised with her weight gain and given her permission to be the underdog. I asked her what she meant and she replied that everyone loves an underdog. This was her belief. She was motivated more by the fear of losing friends than gaining a smaller dress size.

The only thing that ever stops us from stepping into our magnificence is fear.

We worked together and I helped Lucy to see that being the underdog was victim behaviour. Her friends' sympathy only served to perpetuate her weight problem.

Lucy came to see why she behaved the way she did, and how her belief system had given her an addiction to overeating and a victim mentality. Her weight problem was the manifestation of insecurity about not being good enough, and a fear of losing friendship. We changed her program. She gave herself the opportunity to see her own uniqueness and started taking responsibility for her own decisions without the validation of her mother. She started to see that there were things about herself to like and be proud of. She relied less on the significance that her friends gave her and saw that this was an inside job. She embraced her uniqueness. Lucy saw that life didn't need to be a competition – she no longer had to benchmark herself against her mother, or anyone else for that matter. It was a joy to see her talking passionately about her new aspirations in life. She adopted a new belief that there is always enough to go around, and that there is plenty of light to shine on everyone. As a result, Lucy's weight dropped steadily. She didn't need willpower, she understood why power. Why her beliefs had encouraged her to overeat in the first place and why she was now worthy of life. She knew which foods would be more kind to her body and health and the ones that were less helpful, and she made it her intention to feed herself with kindness. Yes, she did lose some friends that didn't like her new empowering attitude, but she noticed that they only ever spoke with dense words anyway. With her new self-worth she attracted new friends, ones who supported rather than sympathised with her. These new companions kept her vibration and aspirations high, and they celebrated her success.

> *All addictions are the result of feelings of low self-worth and lack of self-love and significance.*

Decide On The Dream

My friend Diane was reading a book on manifestation and it explained that there are only three ways to co-create anything in your life. The theory was simple: *Ask, believe, receive.*

This is based on the law of attraction – like attracts like, so what you focus on is what you get. The instructions in the book said that if you want something you need to ask for it first. Secondly, you need to have an inner trust that it will manifest and thirdly, you need to sit with that inner trust and wait to receive it.

Diane decided to test the theory out. She asked for something and maintained a faith that it would manifest...

And she waited.

And waited some more.

And nothing happened.

Zilch, nada, nothing!

She was adamant that the law of attraction didn't work. It was all flaky nonsense.

Some weeks later, Diane and I went out on a girly evening with friends. She thought she would try it one more time and asked our friends to join in with the experiment to see if they had any more luck. She posed the question, *"If all you had to do was 'ask' and 'believe' in order to 'receive' what would you ask for?"*

Our friends were very verbal. Everyone shouted out at the same time. Their answers ranged from wanting less stress, anxiety, frustration, tiredness, discomfort, ailments and hormonal swings to putting an end to a fractious relationship, family aggro, financial worries and excessive work deadlines.

Every woman had a big long list and it was absolutely evident that every one of them had a clear idea of...

What they DIDN'T want!

So we started again. What do you really want in life? If you could have anything, what would it really be?

This time their responses ranged from winning the lottery and bagging a toyboy lover to getting a pair of Jimmy Choos, a Mulberry handbag and a Mercedes convertible, and so on, but beyond these immediate desires it was less easy for them to be specific about the bigger picture, i.e., what they wanted in terms of health and wellness, happiness and love and wealth and abundance.

This got me thinking. *How is it that we can be so clear on what we don't want, yet so vague on what we do want?*

Q. ***Do you focus on what you don't want, or have you got absolute clarity on what you DO want?***

RAS

Do you remember that at the start of this book I mentioned synchronicities? I kept noticing feathers and other objects that reminded me of an association with warriors. I compared it to ordering a shiny, new car and then seeing the exact make, model and colour everywhere on the road. How come everyone just went and bought the same car as you?

Q. Has that happened to you?

The ask/believe/receive theory always works, but the key is to focus on what you do want. Diane realised that the theory hadn't worked for her simply because she'd been focusing on all the things she *didn't want.*

It's vital you set your internal Sat Nav so it knows where your intended destination is – your dream. Otherwise all roads lead to anywhere.

There is a part of your brain that will help you accomplish your dream because when you tell it what you are looking for, just like a Sat Nav, it will search for a signal and connect the roads together for the route you need to take. That part of the brain is called your *reticular activating system (RAS)*, an automatic mechanism inside of your brain that will look for information that is aligned with your desires and dreams. But just like the Sat Nav in your car, you need to give it a destination. When good stuff aligns with our desires we often call it luck, coincidence or synchronicity. But it isn't. The law of attraction will present you with opportunities or people that will conspire to help you join your metaphorical roads together. You just need to be specific. When you understand how your RAS works, anything is possible.

Q. What is your intention or dream for life?

Have you heard people say, *"I just go with the flow of life?"*

I'd agree that going with the flow of life can make things easier but here's the thing - going with the flow without a clear intention will not present you with as many opportunities, people and gifts to enrich your life simply because your RAS doesn't know what it is you are looking for. Any road will do.

Unless you specify your destination, your RAS won't know how to help you.

> *Once you become clear about the destination of your*
> *dream you will start to see synchronicities ~ these*
> *are signs that your dream is coming closer to you.*

Playing Your DVD

In the group workshops and seminars I run we use the *DVD technique* to kick-start the manifestation of your dream.

Your DVD is unique. You're the only one who owns it and you have an absolute passion for possessing it. I want you to always feel excited, contented or fulfilled by your DVD. *What is your DVD?*

   ★ **D** stands for **Dream**

As I said before, be clear about what it is you want in life and don't focus on what you don't want. Be specific about your desire. You'll have heard the phrase *"be careful what you wish for"*. Remember, your subconscious program is the obliging servant. It will harvest the seeds your conscious mind plants. For example, don't say: *"I don't want this rusty old nail of a car any longer."* Instead, replace your 'ask' with: *"I want a reliable, comfortable and stylish car."* Here's another example. Don't say: *"I don't want confrontation and aggro in my relationship."* Instead, ask for more *"harmony and respect"*. Focus on the positive. If you focus on what you don't want, your RAS will automatically oblige and find more of it for you – more rust, more aggro. Which is OK if that's what you really want of course!

Consider this. If you focus on a *lack of money,* your RAS will keep reminding you that money is scarce.

   ★ **V** stands for **Visualise**

You must be able to see your dream in your mind's eye. Let's put the DVD in the player and watch the movie of your dream life. Sit comfortably, press play and be the observer of you. As you watch, notice where you are and what is around you. What do you look like?

What are you wearing? What does your hair look like? What is the expression on your face? How are you standing? Are you carrying an inner confidence and trust? Do you feel like the cat that just got the cream?

This time, switch seats. Jump right in and be you in the DVD right there on the big screen. So now you are not watching the movie, you are its star. Touch the clothes you are wearing. Touch your hair and face. See all that is around you in this scene. Know how you are feeling. How are the other people in this scene responding to you? What are they saying? Feel your inner smile of contentment, passion, love and fulfilment.

Everyone can visualise. The challenge is, in your busy life, to give yourself time and permission. If you gave yourself permission, what would you allow yourself to see in your DVD? Who would you allow yourself to be?

★ The final **D** stands for **Detail**

Make your dream come alive in your mind's eye. Create a visual picture that is as vivid and colourful as possible. For example, if your desire is to own a reliable, comfortable and stylish car, then give it detail. What colour is it? What is the colour of the upholstery inside? Is it a hard top or a convertible? Does it have two doors, four doors? Is it a hatchback? How does the steering wheel look in your hands? How does it feel? Does the car have a smell? How does the stereo sound? How easy is the gear change?

Perhaps your desire is a new home. What does the front door look like and what colour is it? Which side is the keyhole? What size are the windows in the house? Are they double-glazed? Are there curtains at the windows? Does it have a driveway? What is the view from the bedroom window? Does the house have a smell? Where is the fireplace? Be specific.

Now that you have the DVD technique you can play out your mind movie. Many people already know this technique, but to make it more powerful and really help it manifest, there is another step.

Next you will learn how to be a **RED Warrior**.

The letters **R E D** stand for **Repetition, Emotion** and **Deserve**

Repetition

In your mind's eye, you need to constantly repeat the vision of what it is you do want. Remember, your subconscious doesn't know the difference between real and imagined. It has no concept of time. It can only operate in this now moment. The more you play your DVD, the more your program will see that you are already in receipt of what it is you desire, and the more it will believe it's rightfully yours. Remind yourself to keep repeating and replaying your DVD. Your RAS will start looking for the roads of opportunity to help you.

The easiest way to remind yourself to keep repeating and replaying your DVD is to have a trigger (sometimes called an anchor). For example, you may want to use a key as your trigger. Let's say your car key. Every time you put your key in the ignition, use this as the trigger to command your new vision to mind. Do it again when you remove the key. Alternatively, put a Post-it note on your computer screen, or set an alarm on your phone. Every time you look at the note or hear the alarm, command your DVD to your mind's eye. The key to success with this technique is repetition, repetition, repetition. Visualise that you already have it. Visualise it when you wake up, visualise it when your head hits the pillow.

Emotion

Next, give yourself some emotion in your DVD. This is really important. How do you feel now that you already have this car, house, holiday? Note that I said now you have already got it, not when you get it. You want to send signals to your subconscious program that you are already the proud owner. Remember, your program only thinks in the present moment. I have used material possessions as the examples here, but the same principles apply for you now that you have commanded a smaller dress size, a new loving and respectful partner, full health, an exam pass, a successful presentation delivery, the sharing of your talent with the world. Really take time to take that feeling into your body. Notice where in your body it is. How does it feel? Do you feel energised, alive, vital, relaxed, free, loved, fulfilled? Remind yourself of this feeling as frequently as possible. Of course, you will have to take some action to make your dream happen but the point I am making here is that everything is a feeling. If your vision doesn't command an emotion of feeling good about the outcome then it's unlikely that your desire will manifest.

Another hint - don't get yourself caught up in the future gap.

For instance, you may say, *"My dream is to be one stone lighter by December this year."*

Now, if I asked you what the outcome of this dream will be you might answer, *"When I have lost a stone, I will wear (do/verb) a smaller dress size and then I will be happy."*

This is known as the **Have, Do, Be** statement. You will *only be...* when *you have...*

Let me give you some other examples:

→ When I have a place of my own I'll be able to do my own thing and then I will be happy.

→ When I have more time I'll do more exercise, lose weight and then I will be healthier.

These statements reflect that happiness, success, health, contentment or relaxation is a future based event - *something yet to happen.*

How about changing the syntax of the words so that they read the other way round? **Be, do, have** rather than *have, do, be.*

What do I mean?

Well, you could take on the demeanour of the person you want to be *now.* See yourself doing what it is you dream of and notice how that feels. Take *that* feeling of happiness, contentment, success, relaxation, etc., into every cell of your body and let it happen *NOW.*

I will remind you that your DVD has to play out as though you have already got whatever it is you want. It is happening now.

Deserve

Lastly, check in with your feelings in terms of how much you deserve this. If you can hear your inner voice finding reasons why you will never have the possessions or the success you dream of, then there's something in your program that is telling you that you are not worthy. If you can hear your own voice of self-sabotage then examine the cause of your doubt; all the occasions that put a ceiling on what you could have and expect from life. All the times you were told, *"you can't have that it's too expensive"* or *"that will never happen,"* or had to accept second best; all the occasions that you were made to feel inadequate, thrown over or disrespected.

Q. How easily can you recall these incidents?

I have witnessed amazing transformations in adults and children who have let go of emotions of unworthiness through a process called *Emotional Freedom Technique.*

EFT, as it is more commonly known, is a relatively new discovery that suggests that the cause of all negative emotions is a disruption in the body's energy system. (I explain more about energy in Part Four.) The process requires tapping the body with the fingertips on specific points that correspond to acupuncture points on energy meridians. It looks bizarre, but typically has quick results, helping to neutralise non serving beliefs, removing the ceiling on what is possible and facilitating true potential.

EFT, the DVD, RED Warrior and Be, Do, Have techniques are crucial to manifesting your dreams – not just material things but your dreams surrounding your health, confidence, career and relationships.

Lisa's challenge

Lisa had to give an important presentation at work to her peers. Her subject matter had the potential to be divisive and controversial. She desperately wanted her audience to see that there was a win-win for everyone, but she was having a crisis of confidence. In her mind's eye, she could see herself fluffing up her words and losing her memory, or, even worse, she could see her peers shaking their heads, disagreeing and leaving the room. I suggested we play her DVD and apply the RED Warrior and the Be, Do, Have techniques.

She did this over and over in her mind's eye until she was at the point where it was the last few words of her presentation. One by one her audience were nodding their heads and smiling. Then they all stood up and applauded. Lisa was allowed to experience how that made her feel - relieved, satisfied and fulfilled - and we locked into that feeling. During the next three weeks she played her virtual DVD over and over in her mind's eye. She could see people smiling and applauding in agreement. They could see that it was a win-win after all.

The time came for Lisa to do her presentation and before she stepped on to the stage, she recalled her DVD and the feelings of relief, satisfaction and fulfilment. Her presentation was subsequently amazing. Everyone saw her new perspective and jumped on board. It was win-win.

Now think of your dream. Is there a little voice that is already sabotaging it? Does that little voice say: *"Who do you think you are?"/"That will never happen"/"You'll never afford that"/"How the heck do you think that's possible?"/"You're too old"/"You'll never amount to anything"/"You're not good enough to have that,"* and so on?

If you can hear those words then we are back at your table legs, which have given you a program that is in conflict with your desires. It is playing out a subconscious program that deep down believes you don't deserve it. A belief that says you are less than worthy.

Your non-deserving attitude is the result of FEAR; fear of losing something. We will come back to this.

 For now, in your journal, give yourself the headings of *Health & Wellness, Happiness & Love* and *Wealth & Abundance*. Now ask yourself: ***What is my intended destination, dream and desire in these three areas of my life?***

Health & Wellness

This may include your appearance, your new dress size, physicality, stamina, energy, vitality and mobility.

Happiness & Love

This may include a relationship with a significant other, friendships, harmonious interactions at work, things that make your heart sing – pastimes, hobbies, adventure, variety, nature and freedom.

Wealth & Abundance

This may include your security, comfort, material possessions, home, vehicle - even handbags and shoes if you want! It includes your bank balance, your work, your ability to pay bills and your financial freedom. It will also include your lifestyle and your ability to spend your time doing more of what you want, where and when you want. It may also include your ability to contribute to others, charity and philanthropy.

 Q. How much is enough?

Under the three headings you have recorded above, on a scale of one to 10, ask yourself how much you deserve them.

Write the answers down in your journal.

> *The Universe wants you to have your heart's desire.*
> *It is waiting for you to believe you deserve it.*

PART FOUR
Energy

There is a thread that links together **C** **c**onsciousness, **O** **o**pportunity and **D** **d**esires. This thread is **E** **e**nergy and weaves its way through your life as a result of your thoughts, beliefs, feelings, intentions and actions.

We all have this energy. Through this Universal energy we are all connected. We are one.

The Universe

When all is said and done, everything is energy.

Do you remember that at the beginning of this book I said that modern day life seldom encourages us to open our minds to align ourselves with the energies of the Great Spirit, God or the Universe in the same way that ancient cultures did? I wasn't referring to a religion as such, I meant simply allowing ourselves to consciously be in harmony with the source of creation, the elements of Mother Earth and the beauty of light and colour. I will call it the Universe. You can find your own word.

How often do you give yourself permission to stand still? I mean really still. I mean consciously aligning your energy, your thoughts and your intentions with the vibration of Mother Earth. Could you give yourself permission in your busy life to stand still for a couple of minutes and really allow her energy into your body to feed and nurture you from the soles of your feet?

So, you may be thinking that this is all a trifle woo woo. Are you still too busy to stop and be still? Remember the self-help book I referred to as the catalyst for changing my life? I told you that the book was hugely inspirational but what I didn't tell you is that I skipped over the last chapter. The author, Dermot O'Connor, started to talk about something called *Qigong*, also spelt Chi Kung. All I saw was an unpronounceable name and some silly movements that I thought looked a bit lame.

After I had gotten over the shame of buying a self-help book, I developed a passion for finding similar books from the same shelf. What I didn't tell you is that the next few books I selected from that shelf all made reference to *Qigong*. What the heck was going on? Was it synchronicity or was my RAS trying to join up some dots for me and connect me to something? Was my intuition trying to get me to listen? Did the Universe have a plan for me?

"What you resist persists."
Carl Jung ~ Famous Swiss Psychiatrist

After reading *eight* books that all mentioned Qigong I figured it didn't really matter if it was synchronicity, my RAS or whatever. I had to trust my intuition (feeling) and know more. I'm so glad I did.

Qigong translates as *'the way of energy'*.

Energy

Ancient eastern cultures have always known that the body is more than just a collection of its parts: arms, legs, head, torso, etc., joined together. If you were to open your mind you may see that in fact you are an energy body, too. An energy that runs in a similar way to blood circulating around your body, except that if you cut yourself right now you wouldn't see your energy - known as chi or qi.

Bear with me if this sounds odd. If energy awareness is new to you, let me explain...

Have you ever been at a party and instantly felt your energy rise when someone walked in, as if their energy has lit up the room? Similarly, have you ever been at a party when the room lit up when a certain person left?

We all have!

It's probable that you can't physically see energy, but your body senses it. Through this energy you can feel uplifted in someone's presence, or you may want to steer away from them because their energy is dense. People like this have the capacity to drain every last bit of energy from you.

Remember that in Part One I suggested that you look at people's demeanour. Now, instead of just looking at the way they are carrying themselves, can you try and sense an energy that they give off? You may be able to sense if they are the sort of person who lights up the room when they come in or when they leave.

This energy (chi/qi) that runs through your body flows via specific pathways (known as meridians), and this is outside as well as inside. You may liken it to an aura that projects itself outside of your physical body and is present above your head, below your feet and all around you front and back like an invisible sphere. This energy is with you all the time, inside and out, and it merges with everything and everyone that you interact with.

Imagine that the pathways of your energy are like a series of motorways that all link up to each other. For example, the M6 joins to the M42, which joins with the M40. Your energy is the traffic on these motorways. We want the traffic to flow freely but what happens if a lorry jack-knifes on the M6? The traffic (energy) stops on the M6 and has the potential to back up the flow on the M42 and the M40...

For us to remain well and vibrant and attract all that we desire, our energy needs to flow as freely and as harmoniously as possible. Qigong, often referred to as 'moving meditation', allows us to balance our energy flow and reconnect to the Universal energies above, below and around us.

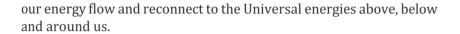

> *The thing that fuels your energy is your feelings,*
> *your emotions. Your body is a field of emotion.*

What if by wearing your coping mask of strength you have, over time, suppressed your feelings: the emotions of grief, anger, sadness, shame, frustration, guilt and fear? What if these suppressed emotions had the capacity to stifle or stagnate your energy flow like a jack-knifed lorry stuck on the motorway? What if these backed up energies had the ability to over flow your stress bath? What if these energies depleted your sense of SELF: your feelings of Significance and Emotions of Love and Fulfilment?

Look around you. Pay attention to the room you are in right now. Look at the glass in the windows and the drapes above them. Look at the style of your chair. Look at the light bulb in the ceiling, or even at a plane high in the sky. Look at this book with its cover and pages. What if every inanimate object had energy?

Everything you can see and touch was the product of a person's desires, dreams and visions. Where did those desires originate? The chair you are sitting on, the book you are reading, etc., didn't materialise without first existing as a thought and an emotion. These emotions then became an intention, which was duly carried out.

Even money has energy. Money is simply the feeling, thought and intention you attach to it.

Let's say you have a £5 note in your pocket. When all is said and done, it's just a piece of paper. The only thing that gives it any value is the monetary figure printed on both sides that tells you it's a fiver. But isn't a £100 note made out of exactly the same paper? In essence, the notes are exactly the same – the only thing that makes one more valuable is your perception of it.

Q. If your face was on a paper note what value would you put on it?

Are you walking around with an invisible energy; an intention that says: *"I'm a big value note,"* or *"I'm a small value note."*

Q. Which would you rather be?

If you are walking around with a small energy value then you may unwittingly be carrying an aura that people sense as a signal to take you for granted, walk all over you, waste your time, blame you and not take notice of your opinion. But remember, the energy you are giving off is simply a reflection or a vibration of the feelings and thoughts you have for yourself. I'll remind you that this is not about arrogance, conceit or vanity. It is simply about giving yourself the opportunity to be kinder to you and to develop a consciousness of what it is you may be inviting into your life through your spoken word and inner talk. It's an opportunity to recognise that your significance is an inside job. What you get is what you tell yourself you deserve.

Nobody can make you feel anything unless your thoughts allow it. Nobody but you is responsible for your own feelings. If someone calls you a loser it may not be nice but that's only because you have the capacity to turn the word into a feeling.

> *The energy you project is simply a reflection of*
> *YOUR FEELINGS.*
> *Are you a high vibration feeling or a low one?*

What if by taking the opportunity to develop a consciousness of your feelings and thoughts you could reprogram your energy? What if, with your intention, you could tell your internal Sat Nav to take you on a new journey, a journey that leads to your dream?

Remember your *RAS?*

Q. Do you deserve it?

Are you sabotaging your dream with your less than positive thoughts and feelings of unworthiness? Do you have a fear of loss or lack, or is there a greater benefit to remaining stuck on the nail rather than living your dream? Is it more comfortable to stay where you are than try to change?

In her brilliant book *'Why People Don't Heal And How They Can'*, Carolyn Myss refers to this as a *'secondary gain'*. For some people, there will always be a perceived gain by remaining in a place of unwellness, discord, unhappiness or poverty because their emotional, mental, physical or financial pain gives them a benefit.

Have you ever met someone who seems to define themselves by their illnesses, trauma or strife because it gets them sympathy or attention? If they were to lose their identity of illness, trauma or strife they would stop receiving attention or benefits from others. For them, there is more to lose than there is to gain by taking responsibility and making new choices. They actually want to remain sitting on the nail; it gives them an external reference for recognition, acceptance and significance. It also gives them an excuse not to step out of their comfort zone and take the responsibility to change. They can rely on other people (an external reference) to give them the significance they crave.

> **"Healing occurs when you see no value in pain."**
> *A Course in Miracles ~ Self study spiritual thought system*

There is no judgment here. At some points in our lives, it's possible that we've all done this. I know I have. We want other people to give us the significance and love we crave. The key here is to have the consciousness when this becomes your victim behaviour. You need to understand that your job ultimately is YOU; your significance, your recognition and your acceptance of who you really are has to come from within. It's an inside job and it starts with the energy – the thoughts, feelings and intentions – that you want to project.

The energy of your body knows how to heal itself physically, mentally and emotionally if it's clear on what journey it's on.

Q. How kind do you want to be to yourself with your thoughts and feelings?

> *"What you say will be the way."*
> *Earl Nightingale ~ US Motivational Speaker and Author*

How Rich Are You?

In 1960, the population of the world was about 3.5 billion. Some 50 years later, it was around 7 billion.

Q. What do you think happened to the wealth of the world during the time the population doubled? Do you think it lessened, stayed the same or increased?

Today, the population is continuing to expand. Do we have enough resources to supply everyone, or are we running out? If you still listen to the news (you might have stopped after reading Part One), you'll be hearing doom and gloom about the recession and economic decline. There is a feeling that we have less and less to go around, and that the cost of living is getting more and more expensive. Let's just examine the truth of this.

During the time that the population doubled, the wealth of the world actually increased 20-fold, even if in reality, inflation meant it only actually went up 13-fold. If economics isn't your thing, then please bear with me. A 13-fold increase won't mean much to you unless you can associate it with the cost of living then and now. £100 today is the equivalent to £7 in the 1960s. But you can buy so much more with £100 today than you could with £7 then. Food is one tenth of what it was in the 1960s, electricity is about one twentieth and transport is about one hundredth. Look at how cheaply you can communicate with people all over the world – often for free. Perhaps you didn't know it, but you are living in the most abundant time in history and yet you may choose to believe you are less than wealthy. You may choose to hear the words recession and economic disaster and allow your program to believe it and feel less than rich as a result. You will see lack and scarcity in your own life because your RAS will help magnify and attract more of it. You may fear that the population is getting bigger and you may adopt a belief that your slice of the metaphorical cake is getting smaller and smaller. Your subconscious starts to believe that there isn't enough to go around.

Q. Is this really true for you? Is your slice of the cake getting smaller? What has this got to do with the vibration of love, fear, self-worth and dreams?

Your ability to step into your magnificence and live your dream becomes limited as soon as your energy - which is just your feelings, thoughts and intentions - focuses on lack, or you have a ceiling on how much you can have. This may stem from a belief that there isn't enough to go around, or that you having it (being greedy) will mean that someone else will not. Or it may mean that you are fearful that having your dream will mean that you will have to sacrifice something else. You are worried that there is the potential to lose something.

Once again, think of your dream. Ask yourself: *Am I in love with this dream or is there a part of me that cannot see it happening?* Your claim on your dream will only be limited by your feelings of FEAR; fear of lack or loss.

These fears might include:

- Fear of losing face or control, which may mean rejection, embarrassment, humiliation, shame or ridicule.

- Fear of losing your health, job, youth, money, possessions, finances or time.

- Fear of losing the love and trust of a partner, friends or family. It may be a fear of rejection, abandonment or betrayal.

How much is enough?

Janice, one of my mates, said that she wished she could win the lottery. I asked her how much would she like to win. She thought about it for a while and then said £1million would do the trick. I asked her why a million. What would a million do for her? She answered that it would give her the opportunity to pay off her mortgage, indulge in a couple of luxury holidays, replace her car, pay for her daughter to go to university and invest some money for a rainy day.

For Janice, a million was enough.

I then asked her if a million was an ample amount to take care of everything she wanted for her family right now, what would having more than that - say £10 million - mean? She looked at me as though I'd gone mad.
"*That's wrong, I'm not that greedy,*" she said.
Then she thought about it one more time, got out her phone and punched a few numbers into its inbuilt calculator.
"*Yes, £1 million would be enough,*" she repeated.

Q. How much is enough?

If you have more than enough feathers for your own nest then feather someone else's too.

I suggested to Janice that if she had more than £1 million, she could still provide for herself and her loved ones, but she could also think of the possibilities beyond that. Once she had provided for her immediate family's needs, she could use the extra £9 million to make a significant difference to others; perhaps people in her own neighbourhood who needed help, or those living on the breadline on the other side of the world. She would just need to think beyond the needs of herself and her loved ones. If she was able to let go of her "*it's wrong to be greedy*" belief, she could buy other people's time to make a greater contribution to all; people she didn't know yet and people she may never personally know.

You'll remember that in Lucy's case, she was afraid of losing her friends and felt that she didn't deserve to realise any aspirations for herself because stepping into her own magnificence would take away the light that shone on her mother. Once she saw that there is no limit, and that there is always enough light for everyone to shine, she had a breakthrough with her feelings of worthiness. She realised that although she may lose the friends that had supported her underdog attitude, there were more than enough new friends to compensate for this.

There is always enough love and light to go around, but it starts with you loving and being kinder to yourself. It starts with you putting your oxygen mask on first.

Q. Do you focus on lack or do you have a fear of losing something?

Remember, I said that fear was a dense, low vibration energy.

Are you unwittingly wearing and projecting a dense energy that might be sabotaging your dream and failing to send you in the direction of people, opportunities and gifts that could help you realise it? Has something made you believe that you only deserve so much? Is there a ceiling on what you can have?

Q. Do you get this yet?

Make Gratitude Your Attitude

 Change your feelings, thoughts and intentions from feelings of lack and fear to gratitude. Set your intention to be grateful. Find three things to be grateful for each day and write this in your journal. These are my 3 things, as I am writing this book.

★ My hands and my ability to type.

★ My laptop to store the document.

★ The electricity that powers the lights – it's now dark outside.

It's possible that in your busy life you have been so focused on what you haven't got that you've overlooked that you already have shoes on your feet, food on your table and clean running water. In some parts of the world that makes you mega wealthy. Be thankful. And the more thankful you are, the more you will see that your cup is overflowing. The more grateful you are, the more your RAS will start looking out for more and more things to remind you how many riches you possess. It'll do this by bringing more into your life. What you focus on is what you get.

Try paying your bills with gratitude. Be thankful that you have the money to do it. As you hand over your payment at the supermarket say *"thank you"* with feeling. Even if your debts are more than you would like, pay your creditors with gratitude that you've had the privilege of borrowing this amount.

See what happens when your *RAS* notices abundance. Let me know by tweeting me @lizkeaney and using #Kindnesscode or by connecting with me on my Facebook page: *'Liz Keaney Kindnesscode Warrior'.*

I want you to know that adopting an attitude for gratitude is not about thwarting any aspirations to have more – quite the opposite. But just for this moment, *be grateful.*

My great friend Sally was telling someone about the work I do. She described me as a *Spiritual Living Coach.*

I wonder what the word spiritual conjures up for you? I know that in my old corporate life, I would have run a mile from anything that was 'woo woo' spiritual. But what is spiritual? Now I know.

Spiritual is just a feeling. It isn't worshiping a god or deity; it is simply a feeling of energy connectedness - a universal consciousness. It's the sense that there is an invisible thread connecting us to the energy of the ground, ocean, sky and everything in between. It's an energy that allows you to feel the toddler's smile rather than just see it. It's an energy that has no beginning and no end. This energy is infinite and through it we are all connected. There is no separation; we are all made of the same stuff, thoughts, feelings and emotions. And if we are all connected then why do we feel the need to compete? We only feel the need to compete because we are driven by fear, which perpetuates a feeling that there is not enough to go around. Not enough recognition, love, time and money.

When we change that fear to courage - the courage to be magnificent - and know that we are good enough as we already are, we can remove competition. We are happy to collaborate because we know there is enough light for everyone to shine. We can join together to spread peace.

I am no saint. I haven't got my feelings, thoughts and intentions perfectly aligned every day – I am not perfect. But as I mentioned at the beginning, that's fine because this is about being magnificent without being perfect. There is no such thing as perfect. We are human beings and being human means that we can make mistakes from time to time. Once we have the consciousness of what we are doing with our thoughts, feelings and intentions, we can change. We can get out the 'red lipstick' and put a cross through our non-serving words, thoughts and beliefs. When we have a consciousness that we are one and start to collaborate, we can start a healing ripple. Jump on board, let's see if we can heal the world.

If there is something inside of you that says peace is not possible then let me ask you: what is your fear? Your only fear is lack or loss; that by sharing love at such a high vibration you will lose something. You believe that there is not enough to go around. If this is what you believe may I suggest that you examine what you are inviting into your life, and maybe start again at page one.

Once we remove fear and *raise the ceiling of abundance* - all that we are worth - we can share so much more with others.

I invite you to read the *Warrior Women Stories* on the following pages. Their personal journeys to universal consciousness may not make easy reading, but through their stories you will sense their Courage, Choices, Clarity, Connection and Collaboration. You'll see how they removed their mask of strength and revealed their vulnerability, and how by doing this enabled them to live their lives in the truth and magnificence of who they are.

They came to understand their program – why stuff happened to them - and they chose to change it because they realised they were worth it.

PART FIVE
Warrior Women's True Stories

Warrior Woman - Jules Mitchell

The blue briefcase

The gift from my husband was a defining moment - a women's blue leather briefcase. My thoughts were *I've made it!* My career at the time was in banking, sales and training, and I had worked my way up from cashier to a managerial position. I was surrounded by successful married Mums. They all aspired to a certain lifestyle...a lifestyle that compared status, cars, houses and other possessions. Unconsciously, I was there too; the blue briefcase was the confirmation. I quite enjoyed the feeling of having a corporate status. I was the major breadwinner, but behind the briefcase I was frantically juggling the responsibilities of a young family, a home and a career. I had two young children under the age of five. There was no doubt that I was capable of spinning all the plates, but, paradoxically, there was a real dilemma of how to do it all: be successful and actually have a life. I vividly remember a woman I worked with telling me that she spent all her weekends doing housework and domestic chores so she could be ready to start all over again on Monday morning. This made me stop and think: when do you have the chance to enjoy your life?

To climb up that corporate ladder required elements of sacrifice and, looking back, I see that I put a lot of pressure on myself to keep all the plates spinning. Not only was I a mother to two young children and running a home nearly single-handed because my husband worked such long hours, but I was also supporting him and my mother-in-law - financially and emotionally - as my father-in-law had severe ill health.

I started to frequently suffer with ill health; I had an iron deficiency that caused me to have numerous fainting fits. Often I'd faint in front of my work colleagues, leaving me feeling as though I was a complete failure. I'd wonder how other people got this far and still managed to cope. Asking for help or finding someone who could empathise just didn't feature on my *'to do'* list. My personal expectations of who I was would never have allowed me to have that conversation. Expressing my feelings or emotions seemed too *'feminine'*, a bit fluffy, and in the corporate field that would have been a further sign of weakness and vulnerability.

Instability creeps in

Gradually, I felt an underlying instability creep in. This began with me not wanting to do anything much at all. I was slowly losing my desire to leave the house and go to work. But I'd force myself to go to the office and would feel really poorly by lunchtime. I'd find myself leaving work early and then I'd end up sitting in my car for hours on end not knowing where I was going or what I was doing. Eventually I went to my GP, who signed me off. His diagnosis was stress and depression. That almost made me feel worse; depression simply confirmed to me that I couldn't hack it. In my eyes, it labelled me as a failure and I felt completely lost for many months. My life was simply an existence; I wouldn't have even been able to describe what state of mind I was in - it was just empty. I refused prescribed medication and felt I was locked in a world almost without feelings. A life of no joy or excitement, but, ironically, I was even feeling low enough to do anything about it. It was a big pool of nothingness, a huge dis-connection to any feeling, anything or anyone. I realised I had allowed myself to become a label in the corporate world, a label that allowed all feelings and emotions to be eroded. I was off work for five months.

I did return to work, but it was suggested to me that if I wasn't ready to take on the responsibilities of my position then I could take the opportunity to leave. I looked more deeply at those other 'successful' women and it became evident to me that they didn't have much in the bigger picture of a life. So I did leave, and felt huge relief. I didn't have to face people and pretend everything was fine anymore. On the other hand, leaving my job did raise lots of questions.

Mental and emotional challenges

The questions became a daily mental challenge for me. *'What am I doing? What am I here for? What can I try and enjoy?'* I knew I wasn't supposed to be a stay-at-home Mum, but what could I do while having a young family?

Ceramic art painting was a hobby of mine, so initially I set up a little business related to this and taught classes. But after a while I found myself tempted back into the corporate world with a job in sales and marketing for a pensions company. Once again, the 'blue briefcase' feeling returned, and the status made me feel important. This feeling remained with me for quite a while. I felt capable and inspired by this job; I liked and believed in the products I was selling. But as sales expectations grew, I found myself regularly filling my blue briefcase with work to do at home and spending my free time trying to fit it all in. In time, I realised I was losing passion for the company I represented and bid my farewells. Once again, I was in this place of questioning. What was I meant to be doing? I had always wanted to teach and follow in my Mum's footsteps, but had ducked out after completing my A Levels. So, for the next three years, with support from my wonderful husband, I retrained and qualified as a nursery teacher. The classroom gave me a real buzz, and I thought that I had finally found my calling. I fully immersed myself in this new profession, and I was thoroughly enjoying my new vocation and the 'softness' it brought to my life.

Then one sunny August day my world suddenly turned upside down. The man whom I'd loved for my entire life, the person who had been my complete rock through every obstacle, was abruptly snatched away from my family and me. My Dad suffered a fatal heart attack at home and never regained consciousness.

I was extremely close to my Dad; he was my protector, my hero and we both shared an immense love of fun and laughter. His loss was, and still is, the biggest void in my life. I still miss him even though more than a decade has passed since his death; the ache is just different now. Looking back at this phase in my life, I realise that losing my Dad not only affected me emotionally, it also altered my perception of emotions. I had such an outpouring of emotion when he died that I couldn't stop crying. I cried and cried, and cried some more. But I recognised that it wasn't just an outpouring of the grief for Dad, it was a total release of the emotional stuff I'd suppressed for all those years. Everything I'd held on to came out. I didn't want to disguise my emotion anymore; I really wanted my children to understand that it was okay for me to cry, and for them to see me crying. Naturally, they wanted to make things better for me, but I remember saying, *"Let me cry, it's good to cry. I'm feeling this overwhelming emotion of loss and anger and I need to let it out. It's not a bad thing. I'm going down the garden to allow myself some time to feel whatever it is I'm feeling, and when I've finished crying I'll come back."* And that's exactly what I did. I went to the bottom of our garden and cried and shouted and screamed like a baby. I knew then that it was a really positive thing for my children to understand that there is no need to judge emotion; if it is there it needs to be expressed!

In my *'blue briefcase days'* I shut myself off from my feelings and my emotions. There wasn't much expression, but there was plenty of suppression! Back then, I didn't understand how the suppression of emotion could affect physical and psychological health. The biggest truth I have uncovered in the last nine years of research into Emotional Mastery is that the physical body is a manifestation of the emotional body; no wonder I was so ill all the time!

I now understand the immense value of giving myself permission for emotional expression, and this is what I finally allowed myself to do when I lost my beloved Dad.

Unexpectedly expecting

And then, a few years after this sad and difficult time, a little miracle happened in my life. At the age of 39, totally unplanned, I discovered I was pregnant. I'd assumed my child rearing days were well and truly over as my children were now 13 and 10. The news made my husband ecstatic with joy but this pregnancy definitely hadn't been on my radar. Here I was, finally thinking I'd at last found my vocation in teaching and now feeling absolutely floored by this unplanned event. I felt like I'd gone through a massive period of discovery; trying to understand who I was, coming to terms with my grief and my emotional expression and finding a career that fitted, and now here I was pregnant. It was a huge challenge to my confidence and it took me three whole months to really accept this new phase in my life.

However, once I'd come to terms with the initial shock of my pregnancy, this unborn child became a bright shining light; a beautiful thing that brought our family closer together. After my daughter was born I decided to take time out to actually enjoy *'being'*. I became a stay-at-home Mum, and this is when my life began to really start to make sense and transform. This beautiful little girl became my 'Awakening'. She opened my eyes to the simple beauty of life. I was experiencing it through her eyes; the eyes of a child. This was a magical time in my life. We explored, discovered, absorbed, learned and created together. Seeing and experiencing life this way helped me take time to really appreciate life for what it was. Through my daughter's eyes I was reminded of the joy in simple things and the beauty of nature. I moved from doing the things I thought I 'should' be doing and discovered that I could do whatever I really wanted. I could actually be in touch with the real me. I had a fresh wonder for every day, and this became a mindful action. I consciously became aware of things and saw just how beautiful they were; so wonderful that I found myself feeling immense gratitude for all that I had. It became instinctive for me to write down all the things I was grateful for. I became very aware of the beauty I was experiencing and started to realise how so many precious moments will pass us by if we don't take time out to really notice them. A reminder of this was when our newest addition started to sit up unaided and our eldest daughter asked me curiously, *"How old was I when I first sat up, Mum?"* An overwhelming feeling of sadness came over me because I realised that I couldn't remember - I didn't know! In that defining moment I realised how quickly we lose sight, don't see, or easily overlook the really important things in life.

New life of gratitude

It was that 'moment' that prompted me to start writing a journal and bring it to life by adding my treasured everyday photos. I found a wonderful outlet for my creative talents and Gratitude Journaling became really important to me; writing about all the little things that happened, the quotes I'd overheard and documenting my completely ordinary life. Without the unexpected pregnancy and the ability to see my life differently, my journey of gratitude may never have started.

Looking back, I also know that losing my Dad affirmed to me the preciousness of every moment, no matter how insignificant it seems at the time.

Having this precious time away from work with my youngest child allowed me the space to ask: Now Jules, what is it you really want to do? I knew I wanted to continue teaching but not within the confines of a school. I now had a fire and a passion to share the things I'd discovered through my *'Awakening,'* and that's when it came to me – I needed to teach gratitude. To begin with I started slowly with my friends in the creative arts arena, teaching them how to make and use gratitude journals. Later, I taught within local education and local authority well-being programs. It soon became evident that I was being recognised for my power to nurture people's capacity to 'stop and smell the roses'. I was the one who could help others capture the specialness in each ordinary moment through a feeling, an emotion or words.

Over the past nine years, I have made it my *'life's work'* to explore emotions – in all their forms, and have had a blast along the way. Studying and qualifying as one of the UK's first *Laughter Yoga Teacher Trainers* has to be one of the highlights of my life. I have also studied and gained qualifications in Mindfulness and Energy Alignment, to try and quench my constant thirst for knowledge on the fascinating subject of *Emotional Intelligence.* I know it's my purpose to share this with the world.

Something in my hair

I still miss Dad, and not a day goes by without me wishing he could wrap those big warm arms around me, but I have an overwhelming knowing that he is still here with me. His passing brought an increased connection to my emotional and spiritual awareness. It opened up my emotional floodgates! Connecting with people *'on the other side'* was something that I had always steered away from. I had been quite fearful of all that 'spiritual stuff', but one day I somehow found myself sitting with a medium to see if I could *'talk'* to Dad. It was extremely profound; the first thing she said to me was, *"you feel like there is something in your hair".* It was true, for several months I had been bothered by a feeling that something was crawling in my hair. I was convinced that I had some sort of infestation. I bought special shampoos but the crawling sensation remained. The medium said: *"You get easily distracted and your Dad has been touching your head trying to draw your attention to what you need to be attentive of."* In his own way, Dad was saying, *"don't be so busy that you fail to see what you need to see."*

OMG!

In his life, Dad worked flat out, full time, six days a week. Every night he came home so tired and, without even removing his coat, he would sit in his rocking chair while Mum put a cup of tea in his hand. After dinner he would return to his chair and fall asleep. Apart from Sundays, that's how he lived his life. Similarly, my Mum's life was busy. She studied for an Open University degree while she was working, bringing up her family and caring for her aging parents. She would get up at 4am to watch Open University on TV, and sit for hours in her bedroom recording on a reel-to-reel tape for reference. I remember her constantly stating that she always had so much to do and, in her mind, only she was capable enough to do it.

I look back at Dad's message and realise that I didn't appreciate its meaning at the time. I loved the gratitude work I was teaching, but I also believed that to make my business successful I had to work really hard. I pushed myself back into a state of 'busy-ness', unconsciously defaulting to the belief pattern I'd inherited from my parents that said you have to work your socks off and kill yourself to achieve and make money. Looking back, there were so many signs. Family and friends were constantly telling me I needed to slow down and that I was doing too much.

OK, I get it now!

The end of January 2010 found me surrounded by an airbag and blood. A car had crashed into me head on. As I waited for the ambulance I recall saying out loud, *"OK, now I get the message. I think you're telling me that I need to stop."* A week later, on a cold foggy February morning, I was at home recovering when my dogs started barking to be let out. It was still-pitch dark so I got up and wrapped a big coat over my pyjamas, pulled on my Ugg boots and grabbed a torch to take the dogs to the end of the garden. As I stood there shivering I could hear something. It was a buzzing. And then it appeared right in front of my eyes - a big, fat buzzy bee in front of me in early February. Instinctively, I knew this must be a sign. I must listen. What is this bee trying to tell me? The buzzing linked the words in my head: buzzy, busy – busy as a bee. I've been too busy, I need to slow down. That's why I had the car crash. But I also knew that wasn't the message I was meant to be getting. There was definitely something else. Rationally, I was thinking, it's just a bee - and then it came to me... *'Just Be!'* As soon as I said these two words together it was a release, and every hair on the back of my skin stood up. Just Be, I don't have to do so many things anymore – I could just start *'be-ing'.* This was so profound for me. I realised that I could stop being so busy and just be absolutely present in the moment, where everything is just how it's meant to be, and I could be the person I wanted to be. I knew then that I had been given the wisdom of my soul. I was no longer afraid to step into my power and share my gifts with the world. One of these gifts is the power of laughter, and this profound tool has provided hundreds of my clients and me with immense healing and insight.

Vibrational energy

Bees are magnets to pollen, which they use to make the sweet stuff, honey. They cannot magnetise to the pollen without vibrating their bodies sufficiently to fly. A bee is one big ball of vibration. Thanks to my bee encounter, I became more in tune with my own vibrational energy and soul wisdom and now share this through my *Buzz Coaching and Mentoring.* I help people identify where they are on *The Emotional Pathway*™, where they want to be and how that aligns with their goals and purpose. We are not just our physical body, we are all a spiritual essence, and the main thing that gives us indication of this is our emotions. So all emotion is good and has value.

We have all accumulated thought patterns and behaviours from early childhood that we can easily assume are our truths and reality. My role as a personal mentor is to shine a light on those *'false truths'* and highlight the ways in which you magnetise your life: the good, the bad and the ugly! I call it *'Rebooting Yourself Back to True Default'*. My clients work with me at a really deep and profound level. They adopt a *Personal Practice™* that is unique to them, and use practical tools to increase their energy, intuition, happiness and wellbeing, and to understand their behavioural patterns. This enables them to have *Present Moment Awareness* and be completely mindful of the choices they make in their life. We can all walk a new path and access true happiness and fulfilment. The first step is the hardest, but on the way we can always collect the honey and appreciate the sweet stuff.

People recognise that they sometimes feel angry, frustrated or sad, but they don't know what to do with these emotions. We have become so conditioned to brush aside our feelings that we are unaware why we have emotions, and how to give ourselves permission to feel them. There is an absolute reason why we are meant to feel emotions, but we pretend they aren't there, bottle them up or explode really quickly and then hope they're all gone. My role is to show you how you can learn to sit with all of your emotions (the good, bad and ugly), accepting them as a simple guidance system to achieving harmony with your true self. We can take time to examine what the emotion really is, understand it and be kind to ourselves with it. Just having awareness of emotions is such a simple thing, but we are conditioned to skim over this profound learning. In doing so we can easily miss out on the wonderful sweet nectar that is our true essence - to Bee Happy!

Warrior Words

'Just Be' absolutely present in this moment. In this moment, everything is just how it's meant to be. In this moment believe that you already are the person you want to be.

www.jules-mitchell.com

Warrior Woman - Angel Alison Ward

Nothing special

I was born the middle of three sisters. My eldest sister was really funny, the youngest was the pretty one, with baby blonde hair, and there was me in the middle: dark haired and *"not much to look at,"* as my Mum would say. I was labelled by my family as *'nothing special'.* I discovered that they were expecting a boy and I was even given a boy's name prior to my birth.

"Alison," they would say, *"no one really notices you. When your younger sister walks into a room everyone stops to notice, she's a stunner, but not you!"* It hurt. From an early age I felt I had to compensate and tried really hard to make people like me. I made an extra effort to try and please others, especially my mother. I'd do jobs around the house, getting up early to take coffee and toast to my parents in bed at the weekends, vacuuming and polishing without being asked to do so. Often, I'd come home in my school lunch breaks simply to do housework. It was my way of trying to get some attention, some recognition. At school I blended in. The teachers said I was no trouble, really quiet. I conformed.

For the first time

It was both flattering and overwhelming when I got to my early twenties and started to attract a lot of male attention. The boys wouldn't leave me alone; I was spoilt for choice. I got attention for the first time and I liked it. But, looking back, I feel sad for the younger me. My perception was to be liked and loved, and to conform. But it was all about pleasing other people. The boyfriends I attracted were very controlling, and although it felt good to have attention, I found myself being told where we were going, what I'd be wearing and how I'd behave. It didn't bother me because this was who I was - a people pleaser. I went along with it.

When, at 25, I met the man who would become the father of my eldest child, it was pure physical attraction. Looking back, my body gave me several signs that we were not an ideal match. I frequently had gripping pains in my stomach before we met, and would find myself really nervous about saying stuff in front of him that he might interpret the wrong way. However, I ignored the feeling that all might not be well and that he might not be all he seemed to be. Six weeks into our relationship, I made the decision to finish it, but then his mother passed away and so, of course, I backed out. It wasn't an appropriate time. But from then on the cycle kept repeating itself. Every time I made the decision to end the relationship I found myself sabotaging my own endeavours and made up excuses about not upsetting him. Before I knew it, six months had passed and I still hadn't told him it was over.

In love with my bump

I had a hospital appointment for a minor operation and while in there I discovered I was pregnant. All of a sudden, I was completely in love with this baby inside me...this baby conceived through making love. As my pregnancy progressed I loved my swelling belly, but it became very evident that my partner was truly repulsed by my blossoming figure. He refused to look at me naked from the front and insisted I keep my back to him in the shower so he could still admire my petite shape from behind. We were never intimate again. And then the verbal abuse started. *"You're too fat, you're rubbish, you can't cook, you can't clean properly,"* and so on. Within a short space of time the verbal abuse also included the occasional slap. It wasn't that I didn't recognise I was being abused, it's just that my need to be a people pleaser overrode it. The abuse simply meant I'd try even harder to get in my partner's good books.

Eventually, I did find the courage to leave him. So then it was just my son and me, and I recognised my true purpose at that time was to be a really good mother. Financially, I would have been better off if I hadn't worked because I could have claimed benefits, but I wanted to work. It added to my little bit of newfound self-worth. It was a part-time job that didn't pay much money, so I occasionally went without food so I could feed my son. Money that should have been provided by his father was not forthcoming – this was his way of controlling me.

Then the phone calls started and they became more and more threatening. I was fearful, especially for the safety of my son. I lived in a haze of sleep deprivation, forcing myself to stay awake throughout the night while he slept so I could be sure he remained protected.

Looking back, I see that I was given signs to pay attention. One of these was a vivid dream in which my ex was going to try and kill me. It was so real and frightening that I went to the police, but without proof they couldn't do anything.

I wasn't looking for another relationship when I met Wayne when my son was two and half years old. Our meeting was engineered by friends, and we instantly felt a connection. Six weeks after we got together we realised there was something really special between us, but we knew we needed to leave things open. Wayne had previously made plans for a 10 week European biking tour with his mate, and this trip had to be honoured. We decided that if our spark was still alive when he returned, we would see how things turned out. The day he left for Europe was July 5 1994.

July 5 1994

I had no idea this would be the day when my son's father would turn up on my doorstep. He had found out that Wayne and I had been seeing each other and as I opened the door said, *"I've come to discuss our son."* As I heard his words my gut instinct screamed at me to tell him to get out, but at the same time my rational mind thought hallelujah, he has come round to be reasonable and provide some financial help. I realise now that I should have listened to my gut instinct, my intuition. He marched into the house and without acknowledging our child, pulled a knife from his back pocket and told me, *"This is the day you are going to die."* Within seconds he'd headbutted me twice. He pushed me to the corner of the room where he started stabbing me viciously in front of my son. Moment later, I felt myself leave my body.

In that space I found myself moving towards a great light. It was powerful and bright, yet it didn't hurt my eyes. As I moved closer to the light I saw a triangle of people, with my Granddaddad (who had passed over) at the front. It was a pure love experience and very peaceful. Granddad spoke to me in a voice I still remember. He said, *"It's not time to go yet, duck,"* and then I was back in my body. Back in the blood soaked living room with my petrified little boy doing his best to get his father off me. As my attacker attempted another stab, I heard someone knocking on the door – it was a miracle. You see, my neighbour worked as a chef in a local old people's home. He had been at work but something intuitively told him he must come home. He felt compelled to trust his intuition and thank God he did; without him, I'm sure I would not be alive. Returning home and hearing my screams, my neighbour phoned the police. Bravely, he came to my door shouting, *"I've phoned the police, let her go. They are on the way."*

There was one last attempt to end my life. He went to stab my chest but I pulled my leg up to defend myself. The knife wound I got there just missed a main artery.

Before the police arrived my ex had already fled, taking my son with him in his car. A newly qualified policewoman heard the call for emergency assistance on the police radio. Her immediate reaction was to ask herself: Where would a potential murderer take his son in this locality? Miraculously, an inner knowing gave her the answer. My son was rescued by the police just in time; he was seconds away from dying as a result of carbon monoxide poisoning. It was another miracle.

I left hospital with severe wounding and bruising. I was left partially deaf, probably a subliminal reaction to prevent me from hearing any more verbal abuse. I felt very physically and mentally unwell. I couldn't help but keep going over the incident, and felt that I should have done more to protect my son. I decided I must have the devil inside of me. After all, a mother is supposed to protect her child.

My son was traumatised. For a long time after the incident, he would try and jump out of windows at night, fearful his father was coming to get him.

Help ~ Self Kindness

I knew I needed help and visited my GP. She ended up crying as she listened to my story, but she had no idea what to do for me. I left the doctor's on crutches; aimlessly, painfully walking the streets thinking if the doctor doesn't know what to do, how am I supposed to deal with it? I walked for hours. I was mentally and emotionally lost. Eventually, I made it home and lay on my bed. My mother came over and held me. I found that as I was lying there, I was unable to respond to her physical touch. I felt totally detached: I didn't feel connected to anyone or anything at all. If someone I'd conceived a child with could do this to me, then anyone could harm me. I knew I was in the depths of my despair, and I felt worthless. But as I lay there, something told me that I also had to be in charge of my life now. Part of me recognised that my people pleasing and compliant nature had nearly ended my life.

It wasn't easy, but I gradually started discovering how I could be mentally and emotionally kinder to myself. It was difficult, but I realised that although I didn't need to blame myself, I had to take some responsibility for what had happened. This was a huge challenge; it wasn't easy to accept that I'd allowed my son's father to nearly kill him. But the more I took responsibility and sought to accept what had happened, the more I realised I'd become a victim because I'd always allowed myself to play the role of one. It was as though from a young age I'd given other people permission to walk all over me...permission that unconsciously said I'm not significant, I'm not worthy.

Our attacker was imprisoned. But life was no bed of roses. He still made contact from jail and for a while I had to take refuge in a safe house. But during this time, Wayne came back into my life. He was wonderful and helped me look after my son. He shared his love, kindness, gentleness and nurturing nature. But it didn't stop me from feeling vengeful towards my son's father. He had initially been charged with two counts of attempted murder, but the court ruled for the charges to be changed to *'unlawful wounding and administering a noxious thing so as to endanger life'*. He was sentenced to just three years in prison, of which he only served 18 months.

A new opportunity

I felt angry and scarred. One day, a friend made a throw away comment and said, *"The best form of revenge is happiness."* That was all I needed to hear. Those words meant that metaphorically I could stick two fingers up at my ex and adopt an inner knowing of *"I can be happy".* It took time. Learning to be kinder to myself meant setting consistent boundaries and new standards for how I lived my life. It was an opportunity to remove myself from being a victim. That also meant taking responsibility and liking and loving myself for who I was. I really needed to start valuing myself.

From that day on, I started listening to my inner voice and developed little tools to like myself. For example, I'd wake in the morning and my inner voice would say, *"look in the mirror".* I'd resist this at first, but eventually I'd force myself to look at my reflection and the voice would say, *"look into your eyes".* I'd find myself saying, *"Oh, you really have got nice eyes. Alison, you are alright."* Within time, by looking in the mirror, I gradually started to accept myself. The turning point came when I realised that people liked me without me having to try to make them like me.

Each morning, I adopted a discipline to be grateful. I wouldn't get out of bed until I could be thankful for something. Similarly, I wouldn't go to bed until I could be grateful for at least five things that had occurred in my day. Rapidly, I started changing my inner dialogue. Instead of saying *"you stupid cow"* or *"it always happens to me,"* I started correcting my thoughts. *"No, it doesn't always happen to me. It used to, but not anymore." "What you did then was a bit stupid, but you won't do it again."* I noticed that by doing this, I became much more conscious of my self-talk, and correcting it became a very mindful action for me. Within time, I noticed how people were reacting to me. At first, some people seemed confused; some found me too positive, which I thought was hilarious. Every time something so-called 'negative' happened, I would naturally turn it round and see the positive. I realised that even the testing things in life are an opportunity to think and see things differently, and are an opportunity to push through fears.

Everything happens for a reason

Wayne and I became a couple and were blessed with a second son after two years together. We both felt very strongly that Wayne should legally adopt my first son, but this was not without challenge. We didn't qualify for legal aid and the adoption process was costly, so we found ourselves severely in debt. This was because my son's blood father had the audacity to contest the adoption. It took all our money and some more for us to fight his counsel. (Ironic, because as a Category 'A' Offender, he wasn't even supposed to have children live with him!)

I found myself crying at the kitchen table; this was a truly testing time. This time, it was Wayne who chose a different perspective. He said, *"Al, all of this has happened for a reason and the reason is you are going to help people. People will be queuing up. You are going to make a real difference to people's lives"*. Back then though, I didn't know how.

When you are recovering from any sort of trauma, pain or angst, you separate from your soul for a while. The way to bring you back is to find something that you can be passionate about. I didn't know this at the time, but after the attack and adoption challenges, I immersed myself in learning all about Reiki. I needed to know all I could about healing therapies. It became my passion.

Bringing you back to *YOU!*

That was then. Now, the culmination of my gifts and my passion for working with Reiki, Energy, Meditation, Healing and Soul Guidance, has transformed many victims' lives. A lot of people don't realise they are victims. If you wake up with that sinking feeling then something in your life is not working and you may be a victim. Or, if you recognise you are making decisions that are not based on your heart's desire, then you are being a victim to something or someone. You are giving your power away simply to be liked, or to garner sympathy or attention. In giving your power away, you don't want to be heard.

We can all be victims at some stage, but so many women don't want to take responsibility for their lives. Victimhood can feel so dense, but it only takes one step at a time to move on. Start slowly by acknowledging where you are, and begin experimenting with energy. Express gratitude by just being thankful - and be thankful even when things don't go so well. Start daring to dream what sort of life you would like to have. Feel the emotions of how that would make you feel and make the description of your life big and colourful. Don't lose momentum. Don't stop dreaming just because your rational mind is asking you how on earth this is going to happen. Don't sabotage your dreams. Write them in a journal and get yourself a trusted friend or mentor to help keep you on track with your belief that you are totally worthy of your dreams.

My book, *'Bringing You Back to YOU!'* is all about how to be kind to yourself through valuing yourself and having a passion for life. You may have a difficulty in your marriage, job, relationship or career, and this always starts with the premise that your situation is a reflection of something within yourself. It requires a lot of honesty and can be uncomfortable. But eventually, with *'awareness work'*, you can start to take responsibility. As soon as you take responsibility, everything changes. Things turn around. It's not about apportioning blame, it's about changing your behaviour and then observing how other people's behaviour to you changes as a result.

When you find your passion you will become aligned to your gifts. To keep in the flow of your gifts you must be kind to yourself and give yourself at least five minutes every day of quiet reflection. This is time to simply be aware of your breathing. After a while, simply being in this quiet time will help you feel more centred. Be conscious of any thoughts that come and go. Don't judge them, just let them pass. If I want help with anything specific, I ask specific questions. For example, *"Is it a good time to be dealing with this venture?"* or, *"What information can you give me regarding this project?"* And then I'll wait. Answers will come. I always validate them by asking for signs that I will recognise. I can guarantee that once you start experimenting with this, you will get signs.

I look at my outer world as a reflection of my inner world, and vice versa. Reflection is huge and it's a responsibility too. When shit happens in life, I will be really honest with myself and take full ownership. I'll reflect and try to be in that higher place of observation, without apportioning blame.

Push through the doors of resistance

Once you have learnt to play with your thoughts, and have seen what works and what doesn't, you will realise that you are the co-creator of your life. The more you recognise this, the more you raise a consciousness of your SELF. If there is pain in your world, there is part of you that has to know you have co-created it. It's the same with poverty, separation and lack.

My dream is for people to see the dark side of themselves without judgement, but with an acceptance. I want to help them create their lives so they are more earnest and more in alignment with love. It's so fantastic when people understand how it all works. *'Bringing You Back to YOU!'* gives you the framework to push through the doors of resistance and see wonderful things start to happen in your life.

Warrior Words

Start with *'acceptance'* and *'forgiveness'*. Accept and forgive yourself then move on to loving and valuing yourself. Through doing this you will put yourself in a place where you will be able to manifest anything you want.

www.angelalisonward.guru

Warrior Woman - Hayley Lloyd-Wilkins

The dream

9/11 changed the world. It directly affected me in my profession because people stopped flying to the UK for their holidays. Revenue decreased and that meant redundancies. After several years of working in 5 star hotel beauty spas, I now faced the prospect of being unemployed. It didn't faze me. I'd always dreamt of having kids and being able to balance family life with running my own beauty business from home.

My fascination with the beauty and holistic profession began when I was 14. I had a part time job working Saturdays and after school in a hairdressers. I quickly saw the positive effects of a new hair do on the women who came to the salon. I listened to their conversations. Even if they'd had a really bad week they'd leave the premises feeling like a huge weight had been lifted. Everything had been transformed.

When I was 18, I went to a ladies' event surrounding the use of colour. We were shown how the colours we wear massively impact on our skin tone and hair. I couldn't believe the positive boost it gave to so many of the women who attended. From then on, I was hooked. I loved colour and how it could transform self-confidence, so I trained with the company. I travelled the country delivering presentations and personal consultations. Although I was young, it was the start of a passionate journey that was all about helping women look good and feel great. It became very obvious to me that looking good on the outside impacted on how they felt on the inside. In my spare time, I attended college to study other aspects of inner wellness and specialised in aromatherapy and reflexology. It gave me a deeper understanding of self-care. After that, I got a job working for an esteemed makeup and skin care brand in a large department store, later moving to an international chain of hotels to work in their beauty spas.

Gift zone

Ladies came to the beauty spa for a release from everyday life. These were busy women who were happy to talk openly about what was going on in their lives: their stress, angst and their insecurities. I was able to help them be in safe space to let go of all that. I felt totally immersed in what I refer to as my *'gift zone'*; delivering a unique therapy experience for them that made them feel better about themselves. It was all about self-kindness and self-nurture.

Working in the spa taught me a lot about the management side of the business; for example, optimising bookings and selling products, but after a while I started to feel frustrated. The business model started to bug me. The spa became all about number crunching and that limited my time, which restricted the mental space for women to really feel their experience. There was less opportunity for me to help my clients really immerse themselves in the nurture they so deserved. The spa became a production line. It was incongruent with how I wanted clients to feel, and it was against the whole interpretation of 'therapy'.

Nevertheless, I remained with the company, and was promoted to work at a prestigious five star spa hotel in Birmingham. This was a different environment, much smaller and intimate, but the reduced scaling meant I wore three hats. I was the spa, leisure and membership manager all rolled into one. Pretty soon, I realised that three hats presented a huge challenge; I was less able to be in my gift zone again. I knew there was security in being employed but nevertheless, I felt uncomfortably comfortable.

An inner feeling

By now I was with the man I loved. We married and both wanted children. After six months of trying with no success, we had tests. Intuitively, I knew that something was not right. We waited for the test results and learned that the problem was on the female side - with me! It was explained that any chance of us having a family would mean me having to undergo IVF treatment. I felt very scared and fearful about this. As the IVF protocol was described, it occurred to me that there was no way I could continue to wear three hats and remain in the best possible physical, mental and emotional state to deal with the treatment. The long hours my job involved could easily compound the stress of the IVF programme. I knew that the only way I would be able to do it all was to leave work and become self-employed. I sensed big changes ahead.

I had a gut reaction, an inner knowing that this was going to be OK. It had always been part of my dream to work from home. I was being presented with an opportunity to live my dream so I took a huge leap of faith and volunteered for redundancy. It was granted and this gave me the chance to turn some of my living space at home into consultation and treatment rooms. It took a while, but everything involved with setting up the business seemed to flow with ease. Many of my regular clients willingly came for treatments and word of mouth provided lots more. My vision of an amazing business that lent itself beautifully to a family life began to take form. I could see myself taking my kids to school, having a couple of client appointments and then being available to pick them up again. I'd be able to arrange what hours I worked around my domestic life. Now all I needed to do was embark on the IVF programme with an open mind and give it a chance.

Roller coaster

Although the perfect vision was always there, what actually happened was an emotional roller coaster spanning seven years. Every time embryos were put back in my body, my inner voice tried to reassure me that I was pregnant, but then the waiting game would start; two whole weeks of hanging on for a positive result. Fourteen days where every spare moment felt like mental torture. I was constantly looking for signs that the procedure had been successful. Those weeks in limbo, simply waiting to find out, were far worse than the gruelling task of injecting myself. With every IVF attempt, I had renewed hope. But, on hearing that it hadn't worked again, I'd tell myself, *"I can't put myself through that again."* But time does heal. In the fullness of time I'd regain my physical and emotional energy, do my best to change my mindset, psyche myself up and say, *"Let's give it another go."*

I vividly remember one occasion, half way through the fortnight, when my period started. In that split second the whole process of a solid two months of treatment was finished. I felt an overwhelming feeling of despair. It was all over. Even though I'd been practising positive thinking and had made dietary adjustments, it was over. Even though I'd had reflexology and acupuncture and made time for me, it was over. I'd done all the right things and it hadn't worked again. To make matters worse, the hormonal drugs I had been given seemed to magnify my feelings and emotions. Each time the loss intensified.

A deep sadness and loss

Equal to the feelings of loss were the huge waves of guilt. I knew it was my body that wasn't working properly, not my husband's. So every time it failed, I went through this massive feeling of guilt and self-sabotage. All in all, we went through treatment five times. I got to a point where I had to have an open and honest conversation with my husband. I had to ask him, *"If your life can only be fulfilled by us having children, do you still want to be with me?"* We had to share the emotions of going through that difficult conversation. Thankfully, we both agreed that our marriage had come along first.

As I approached my fortieth birthday, I thought I might give it one last try. But when I reached that milestone, I knew that enough was enough. I felt unwell and my father had not long passed away. It was a tough time, and I couldn't go through it again. My rational mind said, *"Hayley, if it's ever going to happen, allow it to happen naturally."* I remember my husband saying, *"If we were not meant to have kids, then there is something else out there for us."* At the time, I didn't know what that might be.

After all I'd been through, my sister announced that she was pregnant (admitting that she'd been scared to tell me). The penny finally dropped during that conversation. I came to the absolute realisation that children were probably never meant for my husband and me. They were no longer part of our life plan. I felt a deep sadness and loss for what could have been, and for the dreams that would never come to fruition, but I knew I'd have to accept it. It didn't happen straight away, but once I allowed myself to step into a place of acceptance it felt strangely poignant. I actually felt grateful that I had my sister and remember thinking, *"Thank God, at least I will have a niece or nephew."*

Within time, I learned that there is a fine line between loss and acceptance so that life can move on. I realised I had to surrender and release my fears for the future, replacing them with faith and trust that everything would work out as destiny had intended. Little did I know that the trigger for *'something else'* would be born out of letting go. By letting go, I realised that it was my turn to concentrate on filling myself up with self-care and self-nurture. I had to be kind to myself. The more I became responsible for my own self-kindness, the more I noticed how many women talk about their guilt. They speak about feeling guilty for all sorts of things that are not their fault, but mostly I noticed that many women share the belief that everyone else's needs must come first. They felt guilty for taking time to be kind to themselves. It was as though guilt was built into their psyche, and it became very evident to me how this reflected in their self-care, self-worth and self-love.

Self love

My own experience made me realise that self-love is the fuel that keeps us going. If you don't fill yourself up first then you are less able to help family, friends or shine in your work. If you don't allow yourself self-kindness and self-care then it's likely, at best, that you will be short tempered with those you love or those around you. At worst, you will feel very resentful. Long term, you will feel more and more miserable.

When I allowed myself to let go of the guilt, I realised that - even without my vision of kids - I'd already had my *'baby'*. I had given birth to a business. This was my gift. It was a business that I loved and it was representative of nurture and self-care: a mind, body and skin experience. It dawned on me that my business had always thrived. It had a business model that matched my ethos and it had functioned even when I hadn't been there 24/7. It had supported me throughout the IVF treatment, and also when I'd taken time out to be with my mother after Dad's death. It allowed me time to spend with my sister after she'd had her baby.

My business had given me the opportunity to take time out for the people that needed me without having to compromise my own time and self-care. Whatever ups and downs life had thrown at me since the business began, I'd still been able to help other women feel good about themselves.

Mind body skin freedom

It became evident to me that my real success had always been my gift of taking women on a journey of self-care and self-love through the power of touch. The self-nurture my clients experienced through my therapies really allowed them time to connect with themselves and feel empowered. It gave them permission to indulge in some self-care. My clients understood that there was no division between their body, mind and skin. Their self-care fuelled their self-love, and in doing so they found the best version of themselves. There was a complete freedom attached to that exploration.

I had a light bulb moment on the day it dawned on me that the birth of Mind Body Skin was my intended baby, and it could help support other therapists who wanted some freedom. I knew this was a gift I could share on a bigger scale. I realised I had created a lifestyle business in which my business fitted around my life, rather than the other way round. This could be replicated and had the potential to turn the traditional beauty business upside down. MBS Partnership had the capacity to nurture on all levels.

I recently read a book called 'A Return to Love' by Marianne Williamson. In it she says, "Before the glorious radiance of the kingdom, guilt melts away and transforms into kindness and will never more be what it was." That was so apt. If I had remained stuck in my IVF story, obsessed with not having a family and never giving myself permission to let go of the guilt, I would never have appreciated that self-love is the fuel that keeps us going. Being kinder to ourselves helps us to share a bigger picture of kindness. It is a freedom.

Warrior Words

Get rid of the *guilt*. Surrender and release fear for your greater good. Have faith and trust. Surrender the past, forgive the stuff that wasn't right and let it go. Find out what you can give birth to and nurture it.

www.hayleylloydwilkins.com

Warrior Woman - Nikki Radvanyi

My Dad

My Dad was a Jew, and he was brought up in Budapest. At the age of 12 he saw his mother marched away by the Nazis. That was the last time he ever saw her. He never did find out where she went, but it was rumoured that she was taken to a concentration camp. From that day on, his life was all about survival. The place he lived became a ghetto, and with every new day came a new risk of being killed. He often *played dead'* until the shooting had stopped and he knew it was safe. Food was scarce but he had untypical blonde hair, which meant that he could hide his Jewish yellow star and merge inconspicuously on the tram with the SS soldiers and travel to the nearest town. Once there he could steal bread or cheese to feed his sister and himself.

Some years later, after the Germans left Hungary, he began his study of medicine; something he'd always wanted to do. But not too long after this, uncertainty once more gripped his country as the Russians stepped in seeking supremacy. He knew he had to get out, leave his country and sacrifice his education. It meant leaving his sister as she didn't want to take the risk, but he wasn't going it alone. Three friends were willing to join the escape plan. They all held the belief that they would be safe if they could get to the Austrian border.

They left in the dead of night. Within hours, Dad found himself shielding his eyes from bright lights shining directly in his face. He feared the worst as the guard moved closer, but his terror turned to relief when he explained he was a friend not a foe. He told them they were travelling in the wrong direction for the border. It was time to turn around and run.

The trio successfully made it to the Austrian border, which meant they were able to eventually get safe passage to the UK. Unable to speak a word of English, Dad found himself in London doing any job he could find. He cleaned or worked as a barista in coffee shops to earn cash and gain command of the language. This paid off and he was able to return to his medical studies a few years later, securing a place at

Durham University. Here he reignited his dream of becoming a doctor.

His troubled past

Around the age of thirty, by now married with two sons, Dad was working as a successful GP in the north-east. That marriage didn't last and after they divorced he relocated to Warwickshire. Some years later, in Birmingham, he met the woman who was to become my mother. She was totally in love with this man. In the early days she was totally enthralled with his history, sympathising with his stories of loss, struggle and survival. He delighted in sharing his troubled past with her. They married and I came along two years later. But in the fullness of time my Mum discovered another side to the man she'd married; a dark side that revealed a very self-centred and cruel person. My Dad believed that he had superiority, especially over women. In his eyes, women were either housekeepers or mothers, simply there to wait hand and foot on men, cook and clean. He used abusive language towards my mother and had no tolerance for me as a young baby that cried. Despite his handsome salary he branded my mother a 'parasite' for assuming that she - even with me as a babe in arms - could live off his money. He insisted she went back to full time employment. My mother did exactly that and, looking back, there is a certain irony because what he really wanted was a woman who was there to look after him and be his housekeeper, preparing breakfast, lunch and dinner at his beck and call. The reality was that my mother became more and more independent and assertive. I admired her strength.

The memories I have of my Dad as I was growing up are of a very difficult man who found it hard to be kind; someone who had difficulty communicating his feelings. He was super intelligent, with a photographic memory, but he really struggled to have personal interaction with people. He couldn't do chit-chat and his social skills were missing. Although he had witnessed persecution many times over he was racist, sexist, ageist – in fact every 'ist' you can imagine. He took pleasure in belittling people but conversely, in an instant, he could just as easily turn on the charm.

Dad was status conscious, materialistic and frugal at the same time. We lived in a huge house with 18 rooms but we weren't allowed to have the heating on; hot water was only for a Saturday. If my mother dared to run the dishwasher without the economy cycle she would find herself in trouble, and I recall him often switching off lights when I was reading. Possessions and wealth were his obsessions. There was no meaning to his life beyond a huge bank balance, owning a flash Jaguar and living in a £500,000 house. He also had the strange trait of keeping his own food cupboard. Only he was ever allowed access to it.

He had no time for people who weren't educated and so, despite his frugality, I went to private school from the age of three. It was while at school, growing older and more aware, that I started to make comparisons. It made me realise that my life was very different. School didn't feel like a happy place. I felt very vulnerable, anxious and self-conscious. But when Dad was there, home wasn't a happy place either. I always had the nervous feeling that I was about to become the victim of his behaviour. He constantly belittled me and made me feel like I was never good enough. I cried a lot.

Like a sponge

It took me until secondary school to connect with some real friends. I bonded with a few of the girls and was able to find my voice in their company, but in the classroom it was a different story. Academically I was very good, but I'd never raise my hand to answer a question because anxiety and self-consciousness always stepped in. I was presented with opportunities to go on stage, dance and do drama but I'd pull out at the last minute because I couldn't face the thought of being seen and judged. I excelled at French and German and got excellent grades, but I remember Dad saying, *"What use is that? You need to be good at maths and science. You need to be a doctor or a dentist."*

Looking back, I was like a sponge and I soaked up his criticism. I had no reason not to believe what he thought of me. I wasn't good enough and in his eyes I was never going to be able to reach my full potential.

At school I went on to get 10 GCSEs and two A Levels. At university I earned a degree and two post-graduate diplomas, but this was still not good enough for Dad. Additional qualifications I got in strategic marketing management and PR were *'namby-pamby'* in his eyes. He'd ask me, *"What use are these to anybody?"* When I got a job, he never congratulated me. His response was, *"What kind of a job is that when you are only earning a chicken shit of a salary?"*

Without a doubt, the most hurtful thing he ever said to me was, *"Who is going to want to marry you looking the way you do?"* This was very painful. I accepted this belief day and night for 30 years, along with the other negative and destructive messages he gave me about not being good enough.

Some years ago, I was reminded how easily these destructive beliefs can be resurrected. By now I was in my 30s and working as a PA. I'd been asked to take the minutes of a meeting and added my opinion to the discussion. In my capacity as the minute taker, having the audacity to include myself in the discussion evidently wasn't what was expected of me. The whole ugly incident was referred to HR. Temporarily, this episode dragged up my *'not good enough'* feelings again. I unconsciously replayed all the times Dad had said there was nothing I could possibly say that would have any value.

Asking for help

I could have let this situation bother me, but by this stage in my life I had a new coping strategy. You see, in about 2001, I recognised I needed help. I needed help with my anger and resentment towards my father. I needed help with my self-esteem, but more than that I had a personal quest to understand why people behave the way they do. I had a psychology qualification and I decided to master an advanced qualification in counselling. This turned out to be one of the most beneficial things I've ever done, and I know everything changed for me when I decided to take that first step. This opened the door and gave me an opportunity to change my life and my future. Prior to this my existence had been one long attempt to please others. The constant effort to please and prove myself affected the way I thought of myself.

It gave me a victim mentality. The turning point was when I realised the only person that could move me away from my victim mentality was me. The counselling qualification taught me an awful lot about myself, but I also realised that this learning is a journey that we never actually finish. We are constantly on a self-development quest, discovering more about self-awareness, growth and improvement. I came to realise there was no point in blaming my Dad for the way he'd treated me. It didn't make his behaviour any more acceptable, but I simply had to see that this was just the way he was. For all his material wealth, he was a very unhappy and depressed man a lot of the time. There was a fear deep within him that something could be taken away from him at any moment. This meant that he could never relax or believe that actually everything was OK. He couldn't let go and enjoy life. He had no way of allowing himself to experience his feelings; he vented what emotion he did have through persecuting my mother and me. As I embarked on the counselling qualification and immersed myself in personal development work, I became able to understand what I needed to know about his behaviour and move on from it. Within time, part of me was able to actually feel sorry for him, but more than that I gained a consciousness of how I was going to live and love my life from now on. This was hugely empowering for me.

Part of my counselling qualification involved real case studies – listening and helping people to be more at peace with themselves. This was a privilege. Some of the people I worked with had life limiting illnesses and being with them really touched me. I remember one lovely lady in particular, and I consider the hours I spent with her some of the most precious ever. She had a terminal illness and as my visits became more regular we got to know each other better. As our professional relationship grew, she felt comfortable enough to ask if I minded her removing her wig. It was an honour for me to think that she felt that uninhibited in my company. After she passed away, her husband sent me a letter, the sentiment of which I still treasure. It talked of the positive impact I'd had on her in the last few months of her life, and how she had kept a card I'd sent her by her side during the last few weeks of her life. This held such significance for me; I realised what I had done had been really valued.

I ended up having a varied career, and in my last job I made good use of my qualifications, working as a PA in marketing and events. But as the recession kicked in, the company that employed me were asking for voluntary redundancies. I decided to seize the opportunity of redundancy and it was granted. Even though it was my decision to leave I still found myself replaying old mental patterning. The little voice inside my head reminded me, *"Nikki, you're not wanted anymore, you don't have anything of value, you're not good enough."* At times, if I allowed these negative thoughts to take over, losing my job seemed like the most horrendous thing in the world. It was a real challenge to discern between the fact that I had chosen it, rather than it being chosen for me. When I allowed myself to look at the situation consciously and more rationally, I could see that redundancy was about the job, not about me personally. So I left the company and went to seek new work. It was not where I expected to find it.

Perfect timing

As I lay there, about to indulge myself in a relaxing massage, the therapist said, *"Nikki, you have got so much skill and expertise, why don't you set up your own business?"* Straight away I dismissed the idea, but as she began the massage, creative ideas started to flow. I started thinking about the different things I could do. I found myself able to connect with my real self-worth and value.

I was about to go on holiday and the therapist said, *"Don't you know, that's perfect timing. Get away from everything. Take a notepad and pen and just let things happen organically."* She was right. When I was away it was just free flow. I couldn't stop. It was like the tap had been turned on and all these ideas came to mind. All my ideas culminated into one big idea. I decided that I could provide a concierge service, a resource for people to go to when they needed an extra pair of hands. It would be just like having a personal assistant; someone who could provide another level of expertise or support that the customer may not have, be that administrative, secretarial, business or organisational.

My concierge business became a reality. It was not an easy transition after having worked in the corporate world for so long. It took me a good year to eradicate any guilt from not pressurising myself to work excessive hours, to be kind and allow time for myself. But now I am my own boss and I respect and value myself knowing that I am making a difference, just like I was able to do when I helped the lovely lady with the life limiting disease. I can focus on what outcomes people really want and use my skills and life experiences to do this successfully. People appreciate my work, but I have nothing to prove anymore. I class myself as a novice entrepreneur but also part of a new energy in business that is being driven by dynamic change makers, a large number of whom are women. These women see the value in helping each other, collaborating in a heart centred way rather than competing. It's fine to be inspired and learn lessons from others but comparison is dangerous. This new collaborative energy is allowing us to let go of our need to prove ourselves; we are safe to share our vulnerabilities in order to grow and learn. This has been a huge shift for me because I recognise that in my younger years I was constantly trying to prove myself to all the people that verbally battered me with hurtful names and words.

Emotional tool kit

So things have changed for me. These days I am a lot more assertive, and I know what I want and stand for what I believe in. I know that it's OK for me to make mistakes because learning from these helps to shape who I am. I know that life will throw me challenges but I have a personal toolbox, my *'emotional survival kit'*, which helps me see things differently when things get tough.

My mother continues to be an inspiration. She is a Warrior Woman in my eyes. Her courage and assertion has rubbed off on me and she continues to encourage me personally and professionally. If I ever find myself with a crisis of confidence or self-doubt I take a look at my CV and remind myself of all the things I have achieved, or I'll reread my client testimonials and really take time to absorb the good things people have said about me and my work.

If my father was still alive, I am not sure if his opinion of me today would be any different. I still don't think he would see the value in what I am doing. But I no longer have any feelings of anger or resentment towards him. I understand that my life is less about what he thought of me, and more about what I think of myself. Self-belief originates from the self. Clearly, he had mental health problems and it's sad to realise that it was far too humiliating for him to ask for help. He would have seen this as a sign of weakness, not a sign of courage.

Celebrate being ME

In 2001, Dad was diagnosed with terminal cancer and despite our difficult relationship, I felt overwrought, finally breaking down six months later. By that time he was on continuous morphine and another side of his personality was revealed. For the first time, Mum and I witnessed a gracious, dignified and courageous man, accepting of his illness and grateful and appreciative for all that we did for him in his final few months. He told us he loved us! It was almost as if he realised it was OK now to let his vulnerability show. I'm glad that he did.

Today, I have fewer worries about the past, or concerns about the future. I am just enjoying now. I value what it is I have to offer professionally and personally, but I am not offended by rejection. I am OK as I am. I celebrate being me.

Warrior Words

Remind yourself that you are *never alone*. There are always people out there experiencing the same thing, or something similar, that you are. The only person who can take the first step is you. Ask for help, reach out and surround yourself with likeminded upbeat people to make your life different.

nikkiradvanyi.co.uk

Warrior Woman - Victoria Warwick-Jones

Early morning start

Everything started to change for me that day. It was 7am. The venue was only five minutes' drive away. Although I felt anxious and really low in confidence, part of me was glad the meeting was so early. If it had been an evening meeting I'd have had a whole day to talk myself out of going. The culmination of everything that had happened in the preceding eight months meant that I'd hidden myself away and as a result my mobile beauty business was waning. I frequently asked myself, *"Should I get a job or shall I try and get my business back on track?"* Deep down, I knew working for someone else was not for me - so self-employment it was.

Networking didn't appeal to me but I met someone who convinced me that a new group in my town was a really friendly one. I could see it was an opportunity to try and get my business going again but I had reservations. Something inside me said, *"Vicky, you must go and do this. Trust it will be OK because if you don't everything with your business will end."* So, somewhat reluctantly, I'd said, *"yes, I'll come".* The evening before the meeting, the organiser phoned me to welcome me to the group and then she dropped the bombshell. *"By the way, Vicky,"* she said. *"Every week we ask someone to share their story about who they are and this week I'd love it to be you."*

I put the phone down and thought, *"Shit, what I have done?"* I knew I couldn't get out of it but I rationalised if people didn't like me I need never go again. I'd never have to see these people a second time.

You can't get your own story wrong

It was about 7.45am and standing at the front of the conference room, surrounded by a sea of unfamiliar faces, I had no idea what I was going to talk about, but I do remember someone saying, *"Vicky, you can't get your own story wrong."*

So I began...

I was only 18 when I had my first child. Like most first time Mums, I had no idea. Post pregnancy, I was really unwell and relied on my mother for a lot of help. My daughter was a very hard to settle child. By the time she was two her father had left us, so I was on my own to bring her up. Her unsettled nature didn't diminish. Every day for her first year at school, she cried and clung to me at the school gates. It was horribly emotional, and once she was there she didn't want to play with the other kids. She was very intense and quiet. By the time she got to middle school it became very obvious that she wasn't happy.

I had numerous meetings with her teachers. My instinct told me to change schools but the staff persuaded me otherwise. They convinced me she was fine, and that they would simply move her to a different class. With hindsight, I should have moved her away. When she was old enough for secondary school it struck me how untypical she was of most girls her age. They generally want to be with their mates, but my daughter insisted on going to a school where no one would know her. In three years at secondary school she only did three days of schooling. She was written off as a truant and naughty. Unfortunately, I couldn't make her teachers see that she didn't deliberately want to miss school; she had a mental health problem that no one could diagnose - and it was getting worse. Her biggest problem was the panic attacks, which started as soon as she stepped out of the car. Before too long they were occurring before she'd even left the house.

Specialist schooling

I managed to secure a place for her at a specialist teaching facility. This was for kids who had health issues that meant they'd miss big chunks of education, or an illness that prevented them from attending mainstream school. It was a nice group of about five to six children. It was supposed to be a temporary measure until my daughter was well enough to return to normal schooling, but she never felt able to return to high school. However, with a smaller class and specialist attention, she was able to cope with her life for the time being. In fact, she did really well. Academically she was very bright and took some of her GCSEs a year early. But eventually the time came for her to leave school. She secured a place at university, but the cycle of panic started all over again. Being away from home and surrounded by lots of people made things start to go wobbly. Typical student life was not for her. Every evening she would phone saying, *"I don't want to go out drinking with everyone. I don't like sharing a kitchen with people,"* and so on. I could only listen and try and reason with her.

Christmas term came. She came home and said she was never going back. It broke my heart. I was so proud that she'd got there in the first place and now I felt despair. Her pattern of panic was starting all over again. She did return to university, briefly, but only to sit an exam that was already scheduled. On the day of the exam she phoned and announced, *"I'm not doing it"*. I tried to convince her otherwise. *"You realise that if you don't do this exam you are pretty much giving up on university,"* I said. She replied, very matter-of-factly, *"I know."* She came home and from that day on, and for months, she did nothing other than sleep, read the odd book and feel sorry for herself. I was frustrated. Nobody seemed to be able to help.

On one particular day her mood was very low. She seemed fragile and depressed. I was at my wits' end. Eventually, she announced she was going out for a walk.

The multi-storey car park

I lost track of time, but maybe an hour and a half later I got a phone call. It was my daughter's friend telling me how distressed my daughter was. She was phoning to let me know that she was on top of a multi-storey car park saying that she had nothing to live for. My daughter had phoned her friend to say goodbye. I shouted at her down the phone, *"Why are you lying to me? Why would you make something like this up?"* Nevertheless, I frantically phoned my daughter's mobile. There was no reply. I panicked and instinctively knew I should take this seriously. I dialled 999 and asked for the police. I heard myself saying, *"I don't know what she is going to do. I know she is very depressed and she is on the top of a multi-storey car park."* The police reassured me and said they'd get someone there, but they needed to know which multi-storey. I had no idea. Her friend had said there was lots of background traffic noise when my daughter had phoned. It was no help. All the multi-storey car parks in the town are on a ring road. All of them would have had traffic noise.

My daughter's number showed on my phone - she was ringing me! I answered and went into panic as I heard a male voice on the end of the line. I listened as he explained that he was a security guard. He had been on the car park rooftop for 40 minutes trying to talk my daughter down. The police and an ambulance had been called and, thank God, for now, she was safe in the security office. I raced there as soon as I could.

Holding on to her tightly, I cried. I cried with relief and cried with frustration that she had felt it necessary to go up there in the first place. At hospital, the A&E doctor treated her like she was a naughty little girl craving attention. I found myself irritated.

It broke me

Her suicide attempt broke me. I was always aware that she was not a particularly happy person, but it totally floored me that she had wanted to take her own life. I had let her down. The guilt rested in my heart. What if she had killed herself? I didn't want to go to my own daughter's funeral. At times I thought I was going mad. I felt the need to be constantly watching her, but at the same time I was asking myself why. If she didn't want to be here anyway, what was the point? I felt really angry towards her, angry that she was prepared to leave me and bewildered that I would have had to explain her absence to her younger sister. I reached out to friends but I sensed they found it hard to understand. Although some seemed genuinely upset, I couldn't help but think they were judging me as an unfit mother whose daughter had felt so desperate she had attempted to take her own life.

She had been this way all her life, clingy and hard to settle. She responded badly to spontaneity, bright lights, stimulation, lots of noise and large groups of people. Self-harming was routine for her. She'd react irrationally if she had no schedule for my whereabouts. Even a trip to the supermarket was a huge challenge. Things had to have some semblance of order and routine for her, otherwise situations would present as chaotic, and panic and anxiety would take over. The medical profession needed to recognise that I'd sought psychological help for the last nine years without success. She had issues that we had no label for. We couldn't carry on like this. We needed help.

At last!

It wasn't easy, but eventually she was diagnosed with *Asperger's syndrome*. I was pleased we had a label but I was also angry. Why had it taken all these years? Weren't the education authorities and medical profession trained to recognise these behaviours? I discovered that lots of information was available, but nearly all of it related to children. She wasn't a child any more. She was 19, a young woman. You can't treat a 19 year old the same as a nine year old. The doctor told me, *"You do know that we can never fix her. All we can do is help her cope with this condition. She needs to learn how to deal with it."*

It was a tough few months. Trying to get her medication right was a struggle and she endured some horrific side effects. At times I felt very scared. Although being my own boss gave me time to spend with my daughter, I recognised that my business was going down the pan as I had so little time to work at it.

Three months later, we were trying to put the rooftop incident behind us. Her medication was starting to have some benefit and we decided it would be a good idea to hire some DVDs, get some confectionary and lounge in front of the TV for an afternoon of laughter, just Mum and daughter.

Looking for laughter

We got to the DVD shop at 11am. It was quiet and only one member of staff was visible. We wandered around trying to choose a film we'd both like, but as we couldn't agree we decided to hire two and were searching for a possible third. We were casually looking at DVDs when suddenly someone was between us, grabbing me around the back of my neck. My first reaction was that it was a drunken nutter, but then I noticed that his face was covered. My next thought was, *"OK mugger, take my handbag."* But then I noticed he was holding on to my daughter too. My maternal instinct kicked in. Oh God, I couldn't protect her. I screamed as he dragged us towards the back of the shop and pushed us into a room. Inside it was an additional masked man and the sole shop assistant, obviously forced in there too. What the hell was going on? We were in a DVD shop, a shop full of empty cases. What on earth were they after? They demanded our mobile phones and started searching frantically through our handbags. I knew my phone wasn't in my bag - it was in my pocket - but it occurred to me that if it rang our situation could potentially be worse, so I handed it over. We were instructed to keep our heads down. I started to panic and could feel an asthma attack coming on – ironic, as only that morning I'd been for an asthma check up at the GP surgery.

We were forced to the floor. Soon it became evident that their objective was to rob the safe. In reality, it was all over very quickly but at the time it seemed like forever. The staff member was locked in a cupboard and we were instructed to release her only after they'd fled with the takings of the safe. The police were with us in minutes and an ambulance was called because my asthma attack was so severe. I can remember saying to the police, *"this shouldn't be happening to us."* I couldn't believe the irony. We had set our intention for a day of laughter and releasing the past, and we had ended up with this. Our clothes had to be taken away and DNA swabs were taken. A female officer took us home and we had to do video statements. Throughout the ordeal my daughter had coped admirably well. She had remained calm, but as soon as we got home she fell apart. Any semblance of normality we'd tried to regain that morning had gone.

Unplug and disappear

Two days later, a Friday, my Granddad passed away and it was then that I really broke down. The events of the past few days and months really hit me. Everything was too much. I could have quite happily unplugged myself and simply disappeared. I felt so guilty. How could I call myself a proper mother? Only three months ago my daughter had tried to take her life and now the robbery. My job as a mother was to protect my daughter. I had failed again.

For eight months after that, I struggled and cried a lot. I didn't like going out. I cut myself off from people. I'd got to the point of asking, *"What else can happen now?"* My GP prescribed anti-depressants. They didn't agree with me and then my hair started falling out. My hairdresser said it was a stress reaction. I was constantly looking behind me. I felt like a victim. I felt sorry for myself, and I was overwhelmed with guilt. Things felt hopeless.

I had been pushed really low, to rock bottom, but I realised that I had a choice. It was either sink or swim. I had to do something. I could either put my hand up and say, *"I need help,"* or wallow in self-pity and stay at home feeling sorry for myself. It took a long time and it felt very intense, but with private counselling and *Emotional Freedom Technique* I learned how to free myself from guilt and stop blaming myself.

I discovered that I had to be kinder to myself by setting boundaries for how I reacted to my daughter's constant demands and, in time, those boundaries started to help her, too. I couldn't allow her to scream and expect me to drop everything and run to her. I had to believe that her world would not end if I was out of the room for an hour, or decided to close the door and take a bath.

After the counselling stopped I worried that everything might revert back to how it was. And in a small way it did. It was easy to crawl back into my shell and I had to keep reminding myself, *"Vicky, you can do this."*

Turning a corner

Now here I was, in front of all these strangers at the 'Vibrant' breakfast networking meeting. Suddenly I felt as though I was taking my mask off. I had turned a corner. It was as though I had said to Vicky, *"It's OK to be you. It's OK to reveal your vulnerabilities."* It felt like I was in a room where everybody understood. The feedback from the group was amazing. They congratulated me for showing the real me. My talk humanised the group; it gave permission for everyone to metaphorically remove their own masks and have the humbleness and courage to say that sometimes business and life is a challenge, and it's OK to ask for help. This united the group.

Having the courage to reveal my vulnerability that day became my strength. It made me realise that life does throw challenges, but it's how we deal with them that matters. I recognised that I'd achieved and coped with a great deal. At that meeting I realised I could be whoever I wanted to be simply by stepping out of my own insecurities. From that day on, I knew I would never wear a victim demeanour ever again. I could be *'good enough'.*

I am not infallible. I am a single parent of two daughters and, of course, I have days that are challenging. I'm not ashamed to ask for help but I ask for help in a positive way. I realise that the Law of Attraction works both ways.

I understand my daughter's condition much more and I know she can lead a normal life. It's just less easy for her than for most young women of her age. She is now at one of the top universities in the country and is doing really well. Relaxation sessions are helping her cope with routine; things like shopping, and working with a personal trainer has taught her that a raised heartbeat is not always a panic attack. Besides, exercise lifts her mood.

I got my beauty business back on its feet, but I found a new desire and passion as a result of networking. I was invited to become a *Vibrant Network Leader* for my area and said yes. I love growing my network area and enrolling new leaders to do the same. I'm proud that we are expanding all over the UK. Being a Vibrant Leader has allowed me to step into the fullness of who I am. It's given me the opportunity to see things differently. On reflection, I see that I'd allowed myself to play small for most of my life. (This was probably not helped by the fact that physically I have always been very tiny and skinny and was bullied at school because of my timid nature and small frame.) In the workplace, I'd allowed myself to feel second-class in many of the jobs I'd had. I never had any sense of self-worth. But now, having taken that first step into the fullness of who I am, I have realised that I am shining. I have realised that I deserve happiness. I am shining and I want to help others to do the same.

My dream is to help and encourage entrepreneurs to talk and connect. I know that had I not taken that first step and attended the networking event, I wouldn't be where I am today.

Warrior Words

Take your mask off. Vulnerability takes courage. Take the first step. Recognise your achievements and shine. Cast off your victim coat and be Vicky-torious! The world is there to be enjoyed.

www.victoriawarwick-jones.co.uk

Warrior Woman - Kaitlyn G Lyndon

Vast Consciousness

My recollection of being a baby is unusually clear. I can remember being on the kitchen table in a cot. I could decipher the room and everything. I also remember being fed and sleeping in my parents' bedroom. Although I had just arrived I was very aware of being a vast consciousness. This was in stark contrast to my tiny body, which made me feel very limited. But although I felt limited, I also knew there was energy beyond my body that extended far greater than the boundaries of my physical form. I had this huge feeling of excitement, a feeling that wanted to propel me into my older self so that I could get on and do what I was here to do, but for now, I needed to grow up first. The only thing that I felt limited by was my physical form and my ability to communicate verbally.

I knew I couldn't yet talk, but I could think. I knew I was just consciousness in another new form. Everything was about getting acquainted with the new, including getting used to how my body worked. I was very aware that I could think something and then do it; for example moving my hands.

I was a much wanted only child to an elderly family of nurses and although they had health and financial concerns I was very aware I was loved. To me that was a natural state. But that didn't last for long.

When I went to school I was bullied. The children picked on me about my different shoes. I longed to wear nice shoes but I couldn't because of problems with my legs. At night I had to wear splints which made it impossible to walk and uncomfortable to sleep. As time went on it seemed like I was bullied for any reason. Life stopped feeling so much fun and frequent visits to the children's hospital became the norm.

I was six when my Dad had his first stroke and this had a huge impact on me and my Mom. He never fully recovered and caring for him meant Mom got very tired. Three years later my Dad died and around this time my Mom was diagnosed with arthritis. Before he passed I remember saying to my Mom *"this isn't the real world; we only come here for a short time and it is like a school."* I didn't need to explain what I meant and my Mom simply said *"yes, I know"* and I knew she knew.

The book

It was one evening shortly after Dad had passed that Mom came into my bedroom. She said *"your Dad was a good Dad; he loved you very much; some never have that."* She handed me a book saying *"this may help you. You will see your Dad again one day."* The book was about a medium called Arthur Ford, who after he died, channelled his words through his secretary Ruth Montgomery. This was an amazing book and giving it to me was the best thing my Mom could have done because it helped trigger my desire to want to reconnect again. The book helped support things that my Mom and I already had a degree of awareness about. It resonated with intelligence inside of me that I found difficult to verbalise. Looking back, it's ironic that I read the book so easily because throughout my school years I'd always had reading difficulties.

When I was eleven, my reading age was only seven. I had a desire to learn but the teachers passed me by. It was easier for me to learn from seeing things not reading books. I hated being in the bottom grade or, at best, the middle grade in an academic system that labelled pupils as 'clever' or 'twits'.

At secondary school I was put in a special class with a great teacher, who said on day one *"those of you who really want to learn - will."* By the end of the year my reading age had improved from seven to thirteen and a half. I remember feeling pleased but at the same time doubted if it was really ever going to be enough to truly catch up. Every year after that I came top of the class.

My school report described me as 'an old head on young shoulders' probably because unconsciously, I wanted to fix everything for everyone; I wanted to do everything I could to help keep my remaining family alive and with me.

Feeling vulnerable

By the time I was twelve my Granddad and various pets had also passed away. My remaining family were in and out of hospital, and approaching teenage years, I decided I didn't love life and everyone in the world as I once thought as a child. I was terrified of my Mom dying and felt vulnerable. I couldn't help but feel different, like an outsider. It was evident to me that I had a very unusual outlook on life and my awareness of this meant that I felt like I was a target. I didn't want to draw attention to myself, so I didn't say or do anything that made me appear too different. I enjoyed finding creative outlets where I didn't have to do something somebody else's way; it meant I couldn't be wrong, in trouble or picked on. At school I really enjoyed English and discovered a passion for words. I loved putting words to paper; poems, stories and songs – the words just flowed. While writing I also got the music that accompanied my words but had no way of writing music down. As time progressed I shared some of what I did with those I felt safe with and on several occasions it was suggested I should become part of a band. The very thought of this ignited something huge within me. A fear of being visible bought back school memories of being visible and bullied.

One day I had a vision, like a premonition. In this picture I was on stage. As far in the distance as I could see there were people in front of me. This vision shook my inner self so much that I immediately stopped writing and doing anything that could draw attention to me. My fear of being visible stayed with me for many years; at times the fear felt so great I felt like a rabbit in the headlights.

I grew up, got married, divorced and did many jobs over the years. Most of my adult working life was spent working as a registered psychiatric nurse and when I wasn't doing that I was caring for family. It often felt like I was on call 24/7.

My Mom passed suddenly in 2011 and my aunt passed in the same year. Their loss left me with a lot to deal with – not just emotionally but on a very physical level where I found myself having to clear two homes in a very short time. Thankfully, the Universe was sending me all the help I could have needed in what felt like the most difficult time in my life. I have great friends.

Being the way I am certainly helped me deal with this; I could sense my loved ones making their presence felt and knew they were still very much here. During their lives they had told me, at one time or another, that it was very important for me to live my life. I felt the best thing I could do to honour them was to do the work I knew I was meant to do.

My fear

The only thing was somehow I had to let go of my fear of being visible. I wasn't sure how but I set intentions to help me trust more. I sent out to the Universe if I am really meant to do this work then make it easy or I am not doing it! At times I could not understand why it felt so hard if it was supposed to be so right. Then I was shown and told things that ultimately confirmed it was all to do with 'Divine timing' so I had to just trust. I started seeing synchronicities and started following what felt right. Little by little I heard myself saying yes to things. I still felt terrified but realised my Soul energy was taking over as I was being told 'this is the right time' - Divine timing.

I found myself at an event where the presenter was talking about life purpose. He asked us to think about what it was we were constantly being called on to do. For me, it was to work with people sharing my awareness and using the gifts I was born with. When he asked 'where are you not showing up in life?' I realised how many times I had said no fearing that if anyone booked to see me I may not be able to do anything, share anything with them.

Not long after this, a lady I had done some rare work for offered to do my birth chart. Reading it she said 'there is something you have to do but it feels so heavy that you almost feel you have got to die to do it'. At the time I thought Yes! This was the first time anyone had verbalised what I had been feeling. I knew I had all this 'other world consciousness stuff' and had been constantly told I was meant to share this but to put myself out there would feel like dying. As the lady said 'the thing I want to tell you is that you will do it and you will be fine because it is what you are meant to do and it is why you are here' I felt a degree of fear lift for the first time.

In 2012 I started to realise from information that was coming through from Spirit that the part of me that was in fear mode was not part of my authentic self. I began asking my Soul energy to come forward as I knew this was the part I needed to connect with to do my work. That awareness and connection made a huge difference and things started to feel much easier, as I was finally being presented with one opportunity after another to move forward. I knew the only way to start sharing my gift was to start saying yes.

I have been saying 'yes' ever since. Standing up in public and speaking was a huge deal for me but as it happens I was fine. No one died! Saying 'yes' still shakes me but I realise that I am just doing what I always knew I was here for. That is, to just be me, my true authentic self and share what it is I know, what it is I can see and sense; to connect with and bring forward my own Soul energy in its truest form and to enable others to do the same for themselves. I am still getting used to these changes and although the feelings of fear are less there is still some way to go. Today I just do it anyway and although I can still feel completely freaked on a very physical level I have learnt that it is totally irrelevant.

People have used the words psychic or medium to describe me, although that hasn`t always resonated with me, although I do work with similar energies, just in a different way.

Doing my work I see that people are weighed down with their stuff of life. Their energy is like a dense vibration that surrounds them. Deep down they know they want to create a different life but they don`t see that doing the same things over and over will only ever get them the same result. Often people are not aware they can make things any better for themselves. We need to create space to make changes on many levels both physically and non-physically – make a gap for a new outcome. In this space saying, thinking or doing something differently can change your energy. You could liken it to de-cluttering, clearing the space for a new energy to flow. By creating a small change of thinking or doing something in a new way allows space to open a door to a new outcome. It can be hard to create change with a full home, full head or full life.

Self-Kindness

It's more important than people realise that in order to make space and to raise our vibrations we have to be kind to ourselves. Self-kindness gives us the opportunity to become more in alignment with our true authentic self. Because our true authentic self is like that – it is love, joy, kindness, it is love in action and love expressed.

So many people are reluctant to give themselves kindness – even a bit of head space by simply turning off the TV or radio which can shut you out of your own thoughts. People often don't give themselves time to listen to the self, time or space to have a new thought, so in effect they stifle their own expansion and it can feel hard to find a new way forward.

Being kind is also about having an understanding of the words we use to describe ourselves. This depends more on the meanings we give to the words we use. Years ago, I would not have thought twice about saying out loud something disparaging about myself, but not anymore. Now, I have the conscious awareness of the energetic vibration this gives out to others. In other words, my description of me fashions the way other people see me, my unseen energy. Being kind is about not harming or hurting yourself with self-criticism, it's about being at peace with where you are – wherever that may be and it doesn't have to depend on someone else's approval. If you can't stop yourself thinking negatively about yourself then at least stop saying it out loud. Every time you verbalise it you are magnifying something that may not be serving your Highest good, but then it does come down to that which you feel serves you whatever that may be, it is all ultimately very subjective.

Creating space

By creating space energetically and doing things differently you give yourself new opportunities for different outcomes and you create space for the new. Different people and things can start to come into your life and we get a clearer idea of where we are at by what we are attracting. Looking at what is starting to manifest can be very interesting. It will be in alignment with the energies we give out, even if we are not consciously aware of it.

The more you come into alignment with your true authentic self the better you will ultimately feel. I can explain vibration like a tower block of flats with a lift to each floor. There is no right or wrong floor. The lift stops at the floor which matches your current vibrations. We change floors by changing our vibrations, so we can change our lives and what we attract at any time, we are powerful creators. The more loving and kind we are to ourselves the better. Many people are not always aware of how to be kinder to themselves and some just don't feel they deserve – but we all do deserve, we are all of value. Our conscious separation from that awareness can cause pain on many levels in life, but everything passes, even that which we find painful. This thought has often kept me going.

Doing what we may feel called upon to do can at times feel difficult, but it can get easier. As you get more in alignment with your Soul energy you naturally become more in tune with your true self and you can't help but feel like you are putting on your own most comfortable and favourite slippers or your favourite outfit, because you are becoming more who you really are.

Warrior Words

Give yourself time and space to be you and to find out who you are. You do matter. Learning to love yourself and life in its truest and most beautiful form is a big part of our journey. Fear is not part of the true authentic self, it is not who we are. I have found it really helps to remember this. My wish for everyone is to love themselves their life and their planet. Spiritually this is a great adventure, it is only our human perception that stops us seeing and experiencing it as such.

www.kaitlynglyndon.com

Warrior Woman - Sue Horne

An inner knowing

It was a February evening and it was dark and raining as I took my usual route home in the car. Even though I'd driven this route many times, I hadn't really noticed the hospice building. But on this occasion I saw the sign outside and something intuitively told me that I would be visiting it soon.

It all happened very quickly, but I had an inner knowing that something was not right with my husband, Terry. We were seldom apart but on this particular weekend, I was in London at the annual Freelance Hair and Beauty Federation conference. On the Saturday evening we spoke on the phone. His words to me were, *"Sue, you're never going to leave me again."* He'd been out that day with his mates having a good time. There was nothing particularly unusual about that, but when he got home he was very sick. Shortly after trying to remove his shoes he collapsed on to the kitchen floor.

That was January 10. From that day on I saw his health deteriorating before my eyes. We needed to find out what was wrong and paid for a private endoscopy. Within two weeks of getting the results we were told that his diagnosis was terminal and it would be months - possibly less.

Terry was my partner, my lover and my best friend. He was the one person I could talk to about anything. But now I really wanted to talk to him and I couldn't. I couldn't find my voice in case my thoughts and fears magnified the situation and made things even more of a challenge for him. He had to find an inner strength to come to terms with what was happening mentally and emotionally, so I needed to find a double amount of strength to remain capable for him as well as myself. I can empathise with any woman who has had to witness anything similar.

The reality of Terry's prognosis was much harsher. A week later he had gone. I was widowed at the age of 46.

I felt anything but strong, but I actually went out on the night he died. I wanted people to know that I had lost him. I wanted them to see that I was upset, but more than that I wanted them to talk to me. It was important for me that people treated me normally. I didn't want anyone to be afraid of talking to me about Terry's life, death and my loss.

The following Tuesday, after his funeral, I went back to work. I knew I needed to grieve but I also realised that I had no choice in this. I had to carry on. It was then that I received a phone call about my Granddad. He had been knocked down and killed while trying to cross the road. I hadn't even had time to grieve for my husband and now this.

Eight weeks later I found myself with an inner knowing again.

This time I was at my gran's bedside; I knew it was her time. I don't know if she heard me but I found myself saying that Granddad and my husband were waiting for her on the other side. The enormity of what was going on in my life was unbearable. In that moment if I could have changed places with my gran so I could be back with my husband I would have done so there and then. But I realised that the only way that was going to happen was by suicide. As I had that thought, an image came into my mind's eye. It was Terry wagging his finger and saying, *"Sue, I didn't do everything I did for you for you to go and do this."*

My husband always wanted me to be OK. Even in his last few days he was telling me what needed to be done to get our affairs in order. He wanted everything to be straight forward after he had gone. He made notes and attached them to the relevant files so that I didn't have to. He sorted out executors, everything. He didn't do all that for me for nothing. In that spilt second I realised to take my own life would be like throwing it all back in his face. It was a massive turning point. I only had two choices – not be here or to make the best of what I had.

The coping mask

For the next 12 months I had to be out and busy. I didn't want to be alone with my thoughts or to hurt any more than I did already. I wanted things to be back to normal.

I was able to put on the mask and pretend everything was fine, but deep down I knew I wasn't OK. After a while I visited my GP who prescribed medication and suggested cognitive behavioural therapy. My relationship with the counsellor felt disconnected; there didn't seem any real benefit so I stopped going after a few sessions.

Sometime later, I found myself listening to a talk show about depression. The guest speaker shared his personal story and spoke candidly about how he had suppressed his emotions of grief after his mother's death. This suppression went on for years and years and he only allowed his emotion to really surface some 20 years later when he faced a relationship breakdown. I listened carefully as he associated the suppression of his emotion with his depressive symptoms. I found myself mentally ticking off all the things he was describing. The only one I couldn't tick was being unable to get out of bed. I was still able to rise in the morning; something in me kept me committed to seeing my hairdressing clients. But nevertheless, it made me think. It was like a little voice that said, *"Sue you do need help,"* but part of me still wondered if I was ready to accept help just yet.

In March, 12 months after my husband had passed I made a decision to join a bereavement group. It didn't happen straight away. In fact, it probably took about six months before I really felt any benefit from being there. Sitting there, listening to other ladies sharing their stories was a help to me. Sharing my own thoughts also gave me comfort because I was having the most irrational ones, and believed I was going mad at times. Being able to speak my thoughts out loud made me realise I was perfectly normal. Having the opportunity to talk and listen helped... and then one day the penny dropped. I suddenly realised that I'd played the role of 'counsellor' for most of my working life as a hairdresser. Of course, my clients came to me to have their hair done, but it dawned on me that the real reason I kept so many regular clients was through my ability to listen.

It was all about support; my clients trusted my ability to empathise and be there for them. I had always privately joked that if hairdressers were on the NHS then people would need less valium! There was no question that being able to talk and get things off their chest helped my clients feel better. It was a bonus that I saw them in their own homes so everything they said was confidential.

After the penny dropped, I decided that there was a new road I'd like to go down. I wanted to build on my counselling skills to help others, but knew it would require gaining a professional qualification. Although I'd run my own mobile business very capably for 27 years, part of me still believed that I was just a 'stupid blonde' hairdresser. I'd left school at fifteen with no formal qualifications. But I amazed myself. I got a place at Birmingham University and proved that I did have academic intelligence. It also made me realise that running my own business for such a significant length of time was a real achievement. I felt proud of myself and my self-belief grew. I learned to play golf and within time I found a new male companion. Inspired by a book written by Shirley Maclaine, we both decided to tour Peru.

A new experience

It was about 2.30pm, and as we reached the Sun Gate of the Inca trail, I could see Machu Picchu and knew I had to get there. Later that afternoon we had a hot spring bath and went out for the evening. Back in bed that night, my body suddenly starting shaking. It felt as if everything inside of me was vibrating. I'd never thought that visualisation was my strong point but all of a sudden I started to see a myriad of colours, and they merged into what I can only describe as Aztec like patterns. Then I saw the most beautiful girl's face. She had dark hair in two plaits. As I looked into her eyes they remained the same but the face turned into one of a Red Indian. Again the eyes remained the same and the face changed - this time into the features of a brown bear. In the bedroom I could hear my friend breathing in his sleep. It was as though I was in two places at once: I was out of my body.

The next thing I knew it was morning. We were up early but this vibration was still in my body.

The coach was ready to move on, and as we were about to leave I burst into tears. I had no idea why and later, as our Peruvian guide toured us round, I had this overwhelming feeling inside me. I tried to be rational, assuming this was because of my menopause or something. And as we moved on these feelings came and went. Later, I went alone into the site of the Priestess House, and without reason found myself crying again. Just then I noticed I wasn't alone; another member of the tour party had stepped into the house with me. We both looked up at the same time, peering through the hole in the roof as the clouds merged to depict a Puma's head. It felt both magical and symbolic - although I had no idea why. I still don't know what that may have meant but I do know that there was something very 'pulling' about that place. I felt a real personal connection, as though I'd been here before. It felt as though the eyes I saw in the girl, Indian and bear were my spirit guides. I've since discovered that the Incas believed that when a person dies their soul goes into the underworld and the puma descends to collect it.

That was in 2006.

Three years later

Three years later, I was diagnosed with breast cancer. I knew from the start that I was going to recover from it and stopped reading the hospital literature about survival statistics. I didn't need to know. Instead I took my mental focus to a client who'd had the same diagnosis 40 years previously: she was still doing just fine. And then I thought about all the other people I knew who had survived. I held the belief it was never going to kill me.

It was an 85-mile round trip for me to get my treatment and my friends were brilliant, transporting me to and from hospital for surgery and radiotherapy. As the treatment reached completion, I wondered how long it would be before I could return to work. The breast care nurse suggested that I could be seeing clients again after about a month. I thought long and hard about work. It was my own business and I needed to make a living, but I made a decision. It felt right to give myself some 'me time' in which to please myself. Mentally, I knew it had to be six months. One by one I let my clients know they'd need to wait a bit longer for me to return to work. Almost all of them understood my need to do this and be kind to myself. I know my inner voice was saying, *"Sort yourself out, Sue. This is time to look after you."*

Broken free

That was five years ago and I feel that I have at last broken free. Earlier this year I attended Liz Keaney's *'Why and Worth'* programme for Warrior Women. It helped me to discover so much more about myself as well as connect and collaborate with some amazing women. Today I feel so much more empowered. I value myself much more and feel really positive about my life. I know that I no longer have to conform to what other people expect of me, and, in setting myself free, I have found the real me.

I realise that everything that has happened to me in my life has brought me to this point. My life experiences happened for a reason, and if through these I can help others feel good about themselves *'outside-in'* and *'inside-out'* then my life has purpose. A while ago I trained as an image consultant and today my business Style your Soul helps women look and feel more attractive through colour and style. My unique approach really helps women to dress to their advantage while maintaining the authenticity of who they really are.

It may be that until this point you have felt your identity has been as someone's partner, mother, colleague or your business card. But perhaps now is the right time to set yourself free, release yourself from conformity and bend the rules around clothes and image while exploring your new edginess. Feel good and comfortable with how you wear your clothes, embrace your uniqueness and know that age is no barrier to how you want to be seen.

My dream

A while ago I had a dream. In my dream I am standing on stage in front of a large group of women and sharing my message about helping women feel good about themselves and set themselves free. In my dream I am amazing, magnificent and authentic, and the other fabulous women that share that stage are, too. I hold that dream strong in my mind's eye. Every day it becomes more real, more awesome and more touchable.

I hope I might get the chance to share my message with you soon.

Warrior Words

Break free. Keep your soul alive. Embrace your uniqueness.

www.suehorne.com

Conclusion

Install your *anti-**VIRUS** programme* - a helpful reminder to keep your energy vibration high and your immunity resilient.

★ V stands for **Vulnerability**

★ I stands for **Invitation**

★ R stands for **Responsibility**

★ U stands for **Understand**

★ S stands for **Student**

Vulnerability is Courage. It's OK to hold your hand up and say that something is not right in your life. It's courage that gives you the willingness to confront your addiction, habit, compulsion or enslavement. It's not weak to ask for help. Ask for other people to help heal your vibration with emotional freedom techniques or energy therapies.

Give yourself an Invitation to maintain a consciousness of your language, your spoken words and inner talk. Invite yourself to notice what is pressing your buttons and be with your feelings instead of suppressing them. Invite yourself to look at the richness of your life. Let go of your feelings of lack and your guilt, shame and blame.

Take Responsibility for the way you feel. Nobody can make you feel anything you don't want to. Ask for help in changing your vibration, but don't give that power entirely to others. You are still in charge of your thoughts, feelings and your intentions. You are still in charge of how you feed your body, nurture your mind and connect with the truth of who you really are.

Understand that your physical body is an expression of your emotional body. Understand that there is no such thing as a bad emotion; they all carry a vibration. Which one vibration do you wear: a high deserving one or a low one? Ultimately, you are your own healer. You need to play a part in your health, wellness, happiness, joy and abundance. *You can do this only by understanding your beliefs and fears.*

Become the Student of your own life. Keep learning from your own experiences, especially the less nice ones. Ask what this situation is trying to tell you. Trust the first answer you receive. Be a Warrior. Trust your sixth sense, your feelings, your heart and mind – your intuition. It will always be right. Find yourself a mentor or a coach who can keep helping you grow, and continue to experience life's riches by stepping higher into your MAGNIFICENCE.

When all is said and done, your life is simply an interpretation of time. Be kinder to yourself and make wiser choices about how you spend time.

Leaving A Legacy

This book is my energy: my thoughts, feelings and intention. So I'd like to share with you my intention and dream. My dream is that through this book and the work I do - speaking and coaching - women will find the courage to be kinder to themselves, to remove their coping mask and their guilt of not being perfect, and, in doing so, become free. Freedom is achieved through forgiveness; forgiving ourselves and letting go emotionally of the guilt, shame, humiliation and rejection we carry, as well as the feeling of being less good, less worthy. Freedom is achieved by forgiving others, not because we condone what they did, but because we understand that whatever they did was done out of fear – a lack of love for themselves. Freedom is achieved through understanding that we are worthy of inner peace.

My dream is to help women see that significance is already within them, not outside of them. I want to show them that self-love has nothing to do with arrogance, conceit or vanity, and in doing so help every woman to step into the magnificence of who they truly are.

My bigger dream is that this book becomes an international bestseller. I say this not because I crave the significance of being recognised as an author (it would be nice, but significance is an inside job), but because with the collaboration of Warrior Women and the KindnessCODE

Community, our cups may start overflowing with personal fulfilment and infinite wealth. When we have this wealth, we can share the millions we don't need personally to leave a legacy to help others fulfil their dreams through the Warrior Women Dreams Database. We can also help abused women and kids who have life limiting illnesses. Once we remove the ceiling on how much we think we deserve, and believe abundance is everywhere, we can share so much with others.

I recognise that God's velvet hammer was just a test to see what I would do with the rest of my life. I have been given the gift of time. I'm planning on being around for at least another 40 years, so I hope I have the pleasure of spending some of that time with you one day soon.

When all is said and done, your life is just a series of seconds, minutes and hours that become years. Don't wait until the end of your life to be kind to yourself. Start today. Step into your magnificence today. You Are Worth It.

Between us, we can start a healing ripple.

My deepest thanks to all the Warrior Women featured in this book, and to those who work with me – past, present and future. I am so grateful to you for having the courage to collaborate with me by buying and reading this book. **YOU ARE MAGNIFICENT!**

Namaste.

Liz Keaney ~ KindnessCODE Warrior

www.lizkeaney.com

About The Author

Liz Keaney is known as *'The KindnessCODE Warrior'.*

She is an Inspirational Speaker, Author and Coach empowering modern women to step into their magnificence by living life more consciously, courageously; with clarity and collaboration.

Her former financial services career spanned almost thirty years until she was diagnosed with cancer, not once but twice, within the space of 12 months. This blessing in disguise forced her to look more closely at her life; her purpose and values and in doing so she unlocked something she refers to as the **KindnessCODE.**

Today, in full health, she specialises in raising awareness of self-kindness and self-worth helping women discover their limitless potential to live a life brimming with health, joy and abundance.

Liz runs workshops and retreats in the UK/internationally where she incorporates her expertise in Nutrition, Naturopathy, Energy Psychology, Emotional Intelligence, Belief Mastery, Mind- Body Intuition and Qigong.

For contact details please visit www.lizkeaney.com

Also available on Amazon *'Self Kindness for Busy Intelligent Women'* ISBN -13:978-1492244929.

What Next...?

Check Liz's website **www.lizkeaney.com** for forthcoming talks and *'Discover your Why and Worth'* workshops. Be a *Warrior Woman* and transform the value you place on yourself and your life, challenge your beliefs and perspective, let go of your need to be perfect and embrace courage, confidence, clarity and collaboration. **BE MAGNIFICENT!**

This is what women have said about Liz's talks and workshops:

Empowering, enlightening and enjoyable. I feel so grateful, so lucky, so happy. Life changing; I can't put a price on that.
Kathryn Watkins-Mbenga

The final day was mind blowing. An eye opening, awesome event that makes complete sense allowing you to explore your own sense of wellbeing and spirituality – and meeting some great soul mates in the process.
Dina Cooper, Family Law Advisor

The opportunity to finally answer the unanswered questions and discover why peace has thus far escaped you. My Heart and Soul are full. I thank you with all my heart.
Jacky Lawrence, 'Back Office PA'

I feel truly blessed. Life changing for me. What a wonderful journey we have all been through...and this is only the beginning. Making peace is as easy or as difficult as you make it. So Excited!
Hang Acharya, Sutton Holistics.

Thank you Liz for giving me the opportunity to step into my magnificence and helping me realise I am actually worth it!! Just so glad to have spent the weekend with such a lovely group – it was amazing; the energy was loving, emotional and incredible and we are all growing thanks to you.
Sharon P

For the 1st time I am able to say 'I am deserving'. Thank you so much.
.J. Shoesmith

Really worthwhile. I have got a lot more out of this day than I have out of any self-help books. It has been a real eye opener for how to get more from life.
Celia Lyne

Thank you for reminding us that it's when we are being unconditionally kind to ourselves that we can stay connected to who we really are and from there, to reach out to others.
Rita H

Inspirational, I now realise the power is within me and I can allow myself to let go emotionally and physically.
Wendy Berol

This was exactly what I'd been looking for to help me. It has showed me why it is so important to work on self-love and the joy of life.
E Higgins

Liz Keaney is an awesome force. Do not miss her events – they sparkle with great energy.
Lisa P

Liz would love to connect and hear from you

Facebook   liz.keaney.9   Liz Keaney Kindnesscode Warrior

Twitter   @lizkeaney   #Kindnesscode

LinkedIn   Liz (Kindnesscode Warrior) Keaney

www.lizkeaney.com